Hilda Tweedy and the Irish Housewives Association

An Irish Housewives Association protest, 1940s

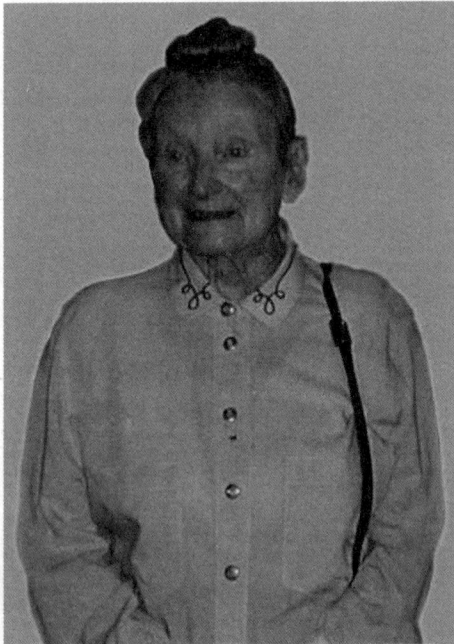

Hilda Tweedy, 2003

HILDA TWEEDY AND THE
IRISH HOUSEWIVES ASSOCIATION:
Links in the Chain ...

Alan Hayes, EDITOR

ARLEN
HOUSE

Hilda Tweedy and the Irish Housewives Association

is published in 2012 by
ARLEN HOUSE
42 Grange Abbey Road
Baldoyle
Dublin 13
Ireland
Phone/Fax: 353 86 8207617
Email: arlenhouse@gmail.com
arlenhouse.blogspot.com
www.arlenhouse.com

Distributed internationally by
SYRACUSE UNIVERSITY PRESS
621 Skytop Road, Suite 110
Syracuse, NY 13244–5290
Phone: 315–443–5534/Fax: 315–443–5545
Email: supress@syr.edu

978–1–85132–033–2, paperback

CONTENTS

LEGACIES

in memory of
Hilda Tweedy (1911–2005)
Andrée Sheehy Skeffingon (1910–1998)

in honour of
all the 'Housewives' who work
for equality in our society

INTRODUCTION

Alan Hayes

> In many ways Hilda Tweedy is the classical example of the more involved older woman ... She has held the most fundamentally radical views on the rights of women consistently since [1941] and never ceased to campaign for them. She is still very radical today, but she is a woman who goes about things gently. Without women like her there would have been no Commission on [the Status of] Women and we would all be a lot worse off today
> – Christina Murphy, 1975

2011 marks the centenary of Hilda Tweedy's birth and so it is appropriate, indeed necessary, for a feminist press and feminist authors to pay tribute to one of the most enduring activists of the past century. In 1986 at the age of 16, I was lucky to have my growing politicisation encouraged by Mary Ryan, my second-level History teacher. Through Mary I met Hilda Tweedy. While she was then in the latter years of her life, she was still clearly a powerful force, and still a gentle woman. Hilda and I talked about doing a new edition of her *A Link in the Chain* which we both felt had not received either the attention or the production values that it deserved. And after her 2003 donation of papers to the National Archives we discussed enriching the book with illustrative materials from the Irish Housewives Association (IHA) papers. Unfortunately time then was not on our side, but I engaged with Catriona Crowe, then President of the Women's History Association of Ireland, and we decided to mark Hilda's centenary. As 2011 came full steam ahead, I decided that a full scale tribute should be done to honour Hilda's life and legacy, in the form of a book, a travelling exhibition and a symposium. These ideas met with enthusiastic responses from the National Archives, TCD, Hilda's friends, the feminist community and the Tweedy family.

The essays in this book are divided into four sections. The first section contains a survey of the continuous activism of the Irish women's movement from the 1870s to the present, a discussion of how women's groups engaged with political establishments from 1900 to the 1940s, and an analysis of women's lives in 1930s and 1940s Ireland. The second section offers reminiscences of Hilda Tweedy and Andrée Sheehy Skeffington, reflecting on their work and influence. The third section examines the work of the Irish Housewives Association in the introduction of rationing during the Emergency; its journal, *The Irish Housewife*, published from 1946–1967, and in its work politicising Irish women. The final section looks at the legacies of these political activists and housewives and the lessons to learn, as we continue the ongoing work for equality, human rights and peace.

The IHA had a wide reach, despite never having had more than 1200 members at any one time. Mary Fitzpatrick (1907–1988), my Rathgar grandmother, was an active member and enthusiastic supporter of the IHA, yet my Baldoyle grandmother, Isabel Hayes (1900–1970), who had 14 births and was widowed young, probably never heard of them.

From the 1940s the Housewives did an astonishing amount of voluntary work in a society that did not encourage the work of female political activists. During this period these young women began their own politicisation and engagment in active citizenship. They were 'on the march since 1942', declaring 'we fight your battles – give us a hand', as they publically 'claimed their right to play a part in the planning for the community'. While their initial work was in consumer protection, they quickly revealed their feminist inclinations and expanded their aims and objectives to 'seek a fair deal for women and children in matters of law, health and education'.

From the beginning their bravery was evident. These were young, married, middle-class women, many with children, yet they had the courage to tackle economic and political forces. In 1942 Hilda and Andrée publically declared that in some poorer areas women were forced in shops to buy other groceries before shopkeepers would sell them essential items like butter, 'this practice amounts to blackmail and must be stopped', they demanded in *The Irish Times*. They deplored the widespread poverty and campaigned for increased unemployment benefits. The following year Hilda was in court against Alex Findlater of O'Connell Street in a claim of overpricing of biscuits.

The Housewives campaigned on an extraordinary range of areas (many of which have resonance in the Ireland of today), from consumer protection, restrictive trades' practices, equal pay, legislation on product labelling, chemists' prescription charges, the 'Buy Irish Campaign', public transportation for OAPs, unsanitary beaches, conditions in slaughter houses, underage selling of alcohol, County Council housing schemes, the cost of school uniforms, and a campaign for all nursing homes to be registered and open for inspection by health and government officials. They joined numerous committees to work on issues of concern to women, children and society. In 1951 Hilda and Andrée actively supported Dr Noel Browne's Mother and Child Scheme. Hilda remembered that at a Dublin meeting:

We [Andrée and Hilda] were shouted off the platform. They shouted 'Communists' and 'Atheists' and even 'Atheistic

Communists' at us and then drove us off the platform while they sang 'Faith of Our Fathers'.

Andrée said that during the period of the communist allegations scores of women tried to join the IHA, but 'we suspected that they were being used to weaken our influence and to weaken our campaigning and so we closed the membership books'. The take-over attempts were virulent and exhausting, and Andrée, who had had a prolonged illness, decided she would leave the organisation.

The Housewives continuously campaigned for changes in the law and in 1955 congratulated two members who succeeded in being the first women since 1927 to have their names included on the list of jurors. They demanded a legal amendment to include women automatically. 'There are many cases concerning women and children where a woman's understanding and experience would benefit all concerned'. They deplored the leniency of sentences given in cases of indecent assault on young girls and expressed grave concern at the increasing number of assaults. From 1961 they campaigned on the marital age (then 12 years old for girls) and asked Government to at least raise it to the Canon Law definition (14 for girls, 16 for boys), but ideally to increase the age to 18 for both sexes. It took until 1974 for it to be raised to 16 for both girls and boys. In 1962 they lobbied the Government on adoptions and inheritance. Hilda was to the forefront in these initiatives. By 1963 they were celebrating their 21st anniversary and, at a garden party, Minister for Justice, Charles Haughey, praised the IHA for 'fulfilling a very useful role in the community'.

Since 1949 Hilda had been working as an unofficial ambassador for Ireland attending conferences of the International Alliance of Women (IAW). In 1961 Ireland was the host, with Hilda and the IHA managing the fortnight long Triennial Congress, with 300 visitors, along with 400 Irish members attending. Hilda publically lamented the small amount of women elected to the Dáil and the low numbers of women voting in elections.

Following an IAW conference in London in 1967, the IHA and the Business and Professional Women's Clubs joined together with other women's groups to set up an Ad Hoc Committee and Hilda was appointed chair. In 1969 she stated that 'women's rights had been considered apart from human rights. Equal status of men and women was necessary for the full social and economic development of our country'. Asked why the committee did not mention birth control, she stated that it was a controversial matter, but should be discussed by the Commission on the Status of Women being established by the Government. In 1972 she was appointed the first chair of the new Council for the Status of Women (CSW).

She was an enthusiastic supporter of Europe, and in 1972 spoke with Dr Garret Fitzgerald TD at a meeting of the Irish Farmers' Association. She was heckled when she said that Ireland would continue to maintain its national character after joining the EEC. Hilda said that people's expressed fears of high prices, of being overrun by foreigners and the loss of sovereignty were understandable, but she felt that Ireland would have more control of its destiny within the EEC. In 1973 she congratulated the Minister for Industry and Commerce for putting 7 women on a new Consumer Council of 15 members. 'We hope in all future appointments to such councils, women be proportionately represented'.

1975 was the UN International Year of Women and major events were planned in Dublin and worldwide; however Hilda Tweedy cautioned that:

> we should not lose sight of the fact that the struggle for women's rights is an ongoing affair … no matter what legislative changes we achieve, the major task will be changing public opinion so that women can be regarded as equal, reasonable, human beings in their own right. Even we women ourselves are inclined to accept the thinking that because discrimination against women has existed for thousands of years, we must accept it … we must

reach every single woman – and man – in the country and encourage them to realise the enormous contribution which women can make to the commuity at large … we want to start something that will not just last for 1975, but which will achieve a real change in society.

Young radical feminists who viewed some of the long established women's organisations as old-fashioned and out of touch disrupted a major conference in Dublin in February. They described the organisers, and most of the audience, as 'middle-aged and middle-class'. Christina Murphy, Women's Editor of *The Irish Times* wrote that the IHA gives:

the distinct impression of being a self-satisfied Dublin clique at this stage – they have country branches, but the national executive is, effectively, the Dublin branch. One must certainly question whether they have made any really sustained effort to give a broader class base to the organisation. In some of the more established older organisations more or less the same women have been involved for 10 or 20 years. Inevitably some complacency and self-satisfaction creeps in – as well as the cabal element …

However, Murphy singled out Hilda from that description:

Some of the older women … are aware of the problem … there was nobody more concerned that the young girls felt excluded at the weekend conference than Hilda Tweedy … and there is nobody more anxious to listen to young people and take ideas from them …

Later that year the CSW organised an ecumenical service, and for the first time women officiated at a service in Christchurch Cathedral to mark Human Rights' Day, 'regardless of creed, sex or marital status'. Alongside Hilda were activists Mrs Eileen Desmond TD, Dr Thekla Beere and Sr Benvenuta (Dr Margaret Mac Curtain). In 1976 in her outgoing speech as Chair of the CSW, Hilda declared:

we must face the more controversial issues in our society – the issues of family planning, divorce, violence in the home, battered wives, battered babies and rape … we must get women to go forward into decision-making positions in every sphere ... we must work to support the women who already hold such posts and encourage many more to go forward to seek office. We look to the just and far-seeking men to support our right to equality of citizenship, so that together we may build a better life.

In 1977 she supported Una O'Higgins O'Malley as an independent candidate in the General Election.

Over the following years Hilda did not shy away from discussing controversial issues. In 1978 she said that it was unrealistic to constitutionally define the 'family' based on marriage. The legal status of illegitimacy was a denial of children's human rights. Divorce and family planning should be open to discussion in a 'freer and more compassionate way'. In 1987 she said that the IHA:

> does not support abortion, but is concerned that the recent ruling in the High Court could have implications which are not realised. This ruling could lead to legislation denying the right of all citizens to information and indeed to censorship. We believe that the right to information is a fundamental and human right and we hope this view would have the support of all citizens.

In a personal letter to *The Irish Times* in October 1992, after the IHA had been dissolved, Hilda wrote:

> I am no advocate of abortion; I do believe in responsible planned parenthood with information and education to carry this out. However, in the case of an enforced pregnancy no woman, or as in the 'X' case, child, should have to carry an unwanted foetus, forced upon her against her will. This is an issue which must be catered for in any caring society. Under these circumstances the choice must be given to the abused woman, or the child and her parents, to do what they consider best in the case of an unsought and unwanted pregnancy.

Hilda Tweedy's life and her legacy present us with many blueprints to follow as we work towards equality, human rights and peace in our society.

The Unbroken Chain of the Irish Women's Movement

Mary Cullen

The nineteenth-century women's movement developed within the economic, political and intellectual developments of the late eighteenth and early nineteenth centuries. The industrial revolution and the expansion of commerce, trade, finance and the professions resulted in the growth of the middle class in numbers and wealth. Middle-class men moved steadily into political office and power, while middle-class women were increasingly confined to what was called the 'private' sphere. At the same time Enlightenment, or Age of Reason, thinking challenged established authorities and emphasised the power of human reason and the equality of all rational human beings. This brought democratic ideas to bear on the long tradition of republican citizenship based on the co-operation of individually free and autonomous citizens to create the common good. Few male thinkers or establishment figures saw Enlightenment thinking as applying to females, but some women could and did use it to support the claim that women were autonomous human persons with both the right and the responsibility to direct their own lives, develop their individual potential and share in shaping the direction of society.

Ironically, the only widely accepted ideology that gave women a mandate for meaningful contribution to society outside the home came from Evangelical religion, itself the result of interaction between Enlightenment ideas and the challenge posed to the Christian churches by the growth of urban populations. Evangelicalism preached a return to an individual Christian life of service, piety and humility, virtues seen as particuarly pleasing in females, and emphasised the role of women as guardians of morality in their family and neighbourhood. It originated in the Church of England but its influence spread widely. The late eighteenth century in Ireland saw the start of an upsurge of female philanthropy. Large numbers of middle- and upper-class women, Catholic and Protestant, moved outside the home into organised action aimed at the physical and moral betterment of the poor, especially women and children. A smaller number became involved in movements such as anti-slavery and temperance, and some went on to organise for women's own emancipation.

The pioneering Irish feminists were few in number and the leading figures appear to have been virtually all middle-class, Protestant in religion, unionist in politics and from backgrounds in philanthropy. A number of reasons are suggested for the absence of Catholics. Historians see the hierarchal structure of Catholicism as less favourable to the development of feminism than most Protestant denominations, with Quakerism the most favourable. Also, philanthropy is seen as an important breeding ground for feminism, and Catholic women's philanthropy, pioneered by lay women, was largely channelled into the new religious congregations during the nineteenth century.

There was an added political dimension. Throughout the United Kingdom of Great Britain and Ireland women shared the same general disabilities under the common law, and largely similar discrimination in education, employment, sexual double standards and political participation. As most reforms required legislation by the all-male parliament at Westminster, there was considerable cooperation between English and Irish activists. To many nationalists the women's movement appeared an English importation, and politically active nationalist women, Catholic and Protestant, were more likely to be involved, as well as in community-based activism, in movements such as Catholic Emancipation, Repeal of the Union, Young Ireland, the Fenians, Home Rule, the Land League and the Ladies Land League.

Starting in the mid-nineteenth century four main feminist campaigns developed in Ireland, running more or less concurrently. Their immediate objectives were: married women's control over their own property; higher standards of female education and access to a wider range of employments; repeal of the Contagious Diseases Acts; the parliamentary franchise. In all these areas men were favoured by law and regulation, as well as custom and generally-accepted sex-role stereotypes.

The issues behind the campaigns interacted with each other. The common law gave a husband complete control of his wife's earned or inherited property, with the exception of entailed landed estate. This directly curtailed the personal autonomy of married women of every social and economic class. Linked with the exclusion of women from higher education and the professions, it made concentration on the accomplishments seen as likely to lead to advantageous marriage appear an economically sensible goal for girls' secondary education. This impoverished education stunted the development of individual potential, and, if women won the vote, would lessen their ability to use it to influence legislation and create a better society. The Contagious Diseases Acts, passed in the 1860s to protect the health of the army and navy, made a woman suspected of being a prostitute subject to compulsory examination and, if necessary, treatment for venereal disease, while leaving the men untouched. They were a tangible example of the sexual double standards operating in both law and public opinion that generally saw women as the guilty and punishable party in sex-related offences such as adultery, prostitution and illegitimate births. The parliamentary franchise was both a right in itself and necessary to empower women to bring the values of nurturing and peace that society associated with women into political decision-making, while exercising the franchise would in itself broaden women's horizons. When the pioneers of modern feminism spoke of women's rights they meant more than equality with men within the existing organisation of society. They meant both the right and the duty to be a fully human person, who developed her individual potential and contributed to making a better society for all.

In the cases of married women's property and repeal of the Contagious Diseases Acts, action in Ireland was essentially part of English-based campaigns. On the married women's property issue, committees were set up in Belfast and Dublin, drawing room and public meetings held, and petitions to parliament organised.. Isabella Tod, a Presbyterian based in Belfast and a leading figure in all the campaigns, was the only woman to give evidence before a Select Committee of the House of Commons in 1868 on married women's property. She explained that the first concern of the Irish activists was the plight of poorer married women in the linen mills in Belfast. Starting in 1870 a series of acts gave married women increasing degrees of control over their property. In the campaign to repeal the Contagious Diseases Acts, meetings and petitions were also organised. Speaking in public on this issue was particularly challenging and politicising for middle-class women who were not expected to know much about issues of sexuality and prostitution, and still less make public speeches about them. The Acts were repealed in 1886.

In educational reform, pioneers like Margaret Byers and Anne Jellicoe established women's colleges, including Victoria College in Belfast (1859) and Alexandra College in Dublin (1866) to provide higher education for women, and educate governesses and teachers who would raise the standard of girls' education at second level. The activists lobbied successfully to have girls and women included in the provisions of the Intermediate Education Act of 1878 and the University Act of 1879 under which the Royal University was set up. These inclusions allowed girls sit the Intermediate Education Board's public examinations, and women to sit the examinations and be awarded the degrees of the Royal University, a purely examining and degree-awarding body. Both inclusions raised standards in female education and opened new opportunities for employment. Women gradually won admission to the degree courses and examinations of the Queen's Colleges in Belfast, Cork and Galway, and in Dublin to Trinity College and the Catholic University College. When the Irish Universities Act of 1908 established the National University of Ireland and Queen's University Belfast, women gained full equality with men in both.

Regarding the parliamentary franchise, suffrage societies again aimed at educating public opinion through drawing room and public meetings, letters to the newspapers, and organising petitions to parliament. On all the issues campaigners lobbied MPs to press for and support bills and amendments to bills or to introduce private member's bills, and Irish Home Rule MPs had a good record of support for feminist causes. The parliamentary vote remained elusive, but in 1896 the suffragists won eligibility for women to be elected and serve as Poor law Guardians. In the reform of local government in 1898 they gained the vote and eligibility to be elected and serve as Urban and Rural District Councillors and to vote in County Council elections. Eligibility as County Councillors did not come until 1911.

By the early twentieth century, considerable, though by no means complete, progress had been achieved in most of the campaigns, except that for the parliamentary franchise. This became a major objective in the first decades of the twentieth century. Now a new generation of young women was arriving on the public scene. They had benefited from the achievements of the pioneering feminists, and were politicised by these, and by the developments in political and cultural nationalism of the late nineteenth and early twentieth centuries, including the Land League and Ladies Land League, the Home Rule movement, the Gaelic Athletic Association, the Gaelic League, the Co-operative movement, the Irish Agricultural Organisation Society, the Irish Literary Theatre and the Abbey Theatre.

In 1900 the first autonomous women's nationalist organisation, Inghinidhe na hÉireann, was founded. From 1908 to 1911 it published the first Irish women's newpaper, *Bean na hÉireann*. The paper advocated 'militancy, separatism and feminism' and argued that gender equality would automatically follow once independence was achieved. The Inghinidhe had an input into the founding of the Abbey Theatre in 1904 and of Sinn Féin in 1905, the first nationalist organisation to have both men and women on its executive. In 1910 the United Irishwomen, still active today as the Irish Countrywomen's Asscociation, was established in connection with the co-operative and agricultural movement. It was politically and religiously inclusive and aimed to stem the migration of young women to the cities by making rural life more attractive.

More Catholic and nationalist women became active feminists. As the suffrage movement grew internationally it adopted new methods, including large scale street demonstrations, with banners, colours and slogans. Some suffragists moved on to what were called 'militant' methods, first to civil disobedience such as refusal to pay tax, then to heckling and disrupting public meetings, and finally to physical violence such as damaging public buildings. This last type of militancy emerged in Britain and Ireland where suffrage had for decades appeared within reach but never materialised. The name 'suffragettte' was coined to designate militant suffragists. The leading militant group was the Women's Social and Political Union founded in 1903 and led by the Pankhursts.

At the the start of the twentieth century the major Irish suffrage organisation was the Irish Women's Suffrage and Local Government Association (IWSLGA). It was founded in 1876 as the Dublin Women's Suffrage Association by Anna and Thomas Haslam, both lifelong feminist activists from Quaker backgrounds. It had changed its name as participation in local government was achieved, and as the campaign for the parliamentary vote expanded. Anna Haslam was now an iconic figure for many young women drawn to feminism. She herself was a unionist but the association was non-aligned politically and included both unionists and nationalists. The IWSLGA was committed to strictly constitutional methods. Many new Irish suffrage societies emerged in the early years of the new century. The Irish Women's Franchise League (IWFL), was founded in 1908 by a group led by Hanna Sheehy Skeffington, from a Catholic nationalist background, and Margaret Cousins, from a Protestant unionist background. Both were nationalist in sympathy. Cousins recorded how the young women went to Anna Haslam, 'the dear old leader of the constitutional suffragists', to explain that they wanted an organisation that was more distinctly 'Irish' and one prepared to use militant methods if necessary. She and they agreed to 'differ on means, though united in aims and ideals'. The IWFL, like the IWSLGA, was not aligned to any political party, though it supported both Irish independence and pacifism. Its membership grew rapidly to equal that of the IWSLGA. From 1912 to 1920 it published a newspaper *The Irish Citizen* under the motto: 'For men and women equally the rights of citizenship: from men and women equally the duties of citizenship'. It was open to discussion and argument and is one of the best sources for the history of Irish feminism of the period. As well as information and debate about suffrage, issues examined and discussed included employment conditions of working-class women and their need for trade union orgnisation; equal pay; domestic and sexual violence against women and children; the need for women jurors, lawyers, police and judges.

The removal in 1911 of the House of Lords' power to veto legislation indefinitely opened the way to legislation for home rule in the near future. Suffragists now had two parliaments to aim at. Unionist suffragists might oppose Home Rule, but, if an Irish parliament was established, they wanted it to include votes for women. For British suffragists, if an Irish parliament gave women the vote, this would strengthen the argument for general UK suffrage.

In 1912 the third Home Rule bill was introduced into parliament with the support of the Liberal government and the certainty that it would become law in 1914. As tensions between nationalists and unionists increased, the Irish suffrage societies maintained unity of action, all agreeing that if Home Rule came it should include women's suffrage. This focused pressure on the Irish Parliamentary Party to ensure women's suffrage was included in the bill. Many Irish MPs individually supported votes for women, but their leader John Redmond personally did not. He also feared support for it might destabilise the Liberal government, thereby endangering the passage of Home Rule, and he imposed a party whip when necessary. In March 1912 a conciliation bill agreed by the major parties, giving a limited measure of women's suffrage, failed to pass the House of Commons because a majority of the Irish Parliamentary Party voted against it. A mass protest meeting of suffrage societies and nationalist and labour women was held in Dublin in June. An agreed statement was sent to all members of the cabinet and Irish MPs stating that, while expressing no view on Home Rule itself, the meeting called for the inclusion of women's suffrage in the bill. When no response came a deputation from the IWFL met Redmond, but he refused to ensure that suffrage be included in the bill.

At this stage the IWFL moved up their militancy from heckling public meetings to breaking windows in public buildings. The aim was to get arrested, brought to court, fined, refuse to pay, be sentenced to prison, in the process generating publicity for the cause. While constitutional and militant suffragists disagreed on methods, the relationship was by no means black and white. Anna Haslam publicly expressed the IWSLGA's disapproval of these actions as detrimental to the suffrage cause, while her private view was more complex. Hanna Sheehy Skeffington recounted how Haslam visited her in Mountjoy jail, explaining:

Don't think that I approve – but here's a pot of verbena I brought you ... the Irish Women's Suffrage and Local Government Association strongly disapproves ... [b]ut here's some loganberry jam – I made it myself.

In January 1913 the Ulster Volunteers were formed to oppose any imposition of home rule on Ulster. In November the Irish Volunteers were formed in Dublin as a nationalist response, and in April 1914 Cumann na mBan was established as a female auxiliary to the Irish Volunteers. Suffrage-First or Nation-First arguments came to the fore among nationalist suffragists. Nation-First feminists argued that Home Rule was the priority and the freedom of the nation would be followed by that of women. The IWFL insisted that suffrage must not be put on hold until independence was achieved.

At the same time some suffragists were interacting with socialism and labour. Some, including Hanna and Frank Sheehy Skeffington, were members of the Socialist Party of Ireland. The Irish Women's Reform League (IWRL), founded by Louie Bennett, linked labour issues with suffrage. The Irish Women Workers' Union (IWWU) was founded in 1911 under the auspices of the nationalist, socialist and syndicalist Irish Transport and General Workers Union, and with the active support of nationalist feminists In the *Irish Citizen* a strong socialist-labour voice argued that working women should not be led by middle-class women, but should lead themselves, organising first to secure better working conditions, pay and opportunities, and then deciding for themselves how to attain the vote. During the 1913 lockout, members of the IWFL worked in the soup kitchen in Liberty Hall, while the IWRL organised support for the families of locked-out workers. When James Larkin and James Connolly founded the Irish Citizen Army in November to protect the workers, women were eligible for membership on the same terms as men.

In August 1914 Britain entered World War I and in September the Home Rule bill passed into law with the proviso that it would not come into effect until the end of the war, and with the question of Ulster to be decided. The war made suffrage activism difficult. In general, societies that supported the political status quo suspended activity for the duration, and put their effort into war work. Many believed that, by taking the place of absent soldiers in the workforce, women would strengthen their claim for full citizenship. The IWFL argued that suffrage activity should continue but found it difficult. The IWSLGA suspended suffrage activism, but aimed to continue feminist cooperation on other issues.

On the nationalist question, Redmond believed that support for Britain would enhance prospects for Home Rule and called on the Irish Volunteers to enlist in the British army. The Volunteers split, with the majority following Redmond's call, while a minority saw in England's difficulty an opportunity for a separatist rising. Cumann na mBan was also divided on the issue.

The 1916 Easter Rising was significant for the suffrage cause. The close relationship between the leadership and Cumann na mBan and the IWFL led to the proclamation's public endorsement of women's full citizenship. It claimed the allegiance of every Irishman and Irishwoman to the Irish Republic and guaranteed 'religious and civil liberty, equal rights, and equal opportunities to all its citizens'. It appears that around 200 women took part in the rising, some in actual combat, others in nursing, cooking, dispatch carrying. The aftermath of the rising brought major losses to the cause of Irish feminism. One was the execution of the signatories of the proclamation, and in particular that of James Connolly, a committed supporter of feminism. Another was the death of Frank Sheehy Skeffington, an active feminist and the editor of the *Irish Citizen*. While trying to stop looting in the city, he was arrested by British soldiers and summarily shot the following morning.

After the rising, as public opinion switched its support from Home Rule to complete independence, Sinn Féin became the political party of separatist nationalism. In its growth and reorganisation republican women were to the fore. Cumann na mBan also grew in numbers. By this time nation-first feminists were less confident than before of their male colleagues' commitment to gender equality, while Hanna Sheehy Skeffington was becoming an influential public speaker in the cause of full independence. Nationalist feminists cooperated in Cumann na dTeachtaire, a council of female delegates set up to press for equal representation of women on all republican bodies. In 1918 Cumann na mBan, the IWFL and the IWWU were active in the anti-conscription campaign, and were joined by the IWSLGA in opposing another government attempt at the regulation of prostitution under the Defence of the Realm Act.

The Great War ended in November 1918 and a general election followed in December. In February legislation had been passed giving the vote to all men over twenty-one and to women over thirty with a property qualification. In November a further act made women eligible for election. Sinn Féin candidates stood on an abstentionist platform and won 73 seats to the Irish Party's 6, with unionists winning 26. Suffragists of all political hues gathered to honour Anna Haslam who cast her vote after over 40 years of campaigning. Only one woman was elected to the UK parliament, Constance Markievicz as a Sinn Féin candidate in Dublin. This was a European first for women but Irish feminists were far from satisfied with Sinn Féin's general support for women's equality, including the fact that it had run only two female candidates, the second being Winifred Carney in a Belfast constituency unwinnable by a nationalist. The *Irish Citizen* gave its assessment of the 'measure of our boasted sex equality. The lesson the election teaches is that reaction has not died out with the Irish party'.

The Sinn Féin members did not take their seats but established Dáil Éireann in January 1919, and declared an Irish republic with the Dáil its constituent assembly. The Irish Volunteers swore allegiance to the Dáil and became the Irish Republican Army (IRA). When the Dáil appointed ministers and departments, Markievicz was appointed Minister for Labour, another first for women, while in other alternative government structures a number of women were appointed to the republican courts.

The War of Independence between the IRA and the government forces from 1919 to 1921 took the form of guerrilla warfare, and Cumann na mBan played a more active role than had been possible in 1916. The importance of their participation was recognised by IRA leaders, and nationalist feminists used this contribution, in conjunction with the 1916 proclamation, to insist on full citizenship for women in whatever political entity would evenually emerge. But the war years were difficult for feminism. A major loss was the demise of the *Irish Citizen*. It had progressively diminished in size and appeared at longer intervals. In the last issue, dated September-December 1920, Hanna Sheehy Skeffington reviewed the position. During the present fighting in Ireland, as in the recent Great War, she wrote, 'the women's movement merged into the national movement, temporarily at least, and women became patriots rather that feminists, and heroes' wives or widows rather than human beings'. Feminism could only mark time and wait. Meanwhile she hoped the paper could survive but to do so it needed a woman's movement and readers and thinkers.

Before the war ended Ireland was partitioned. The Government of Ireland Act of 1920 repealed the 1914 Home Rule Act and established two devolved parliaments in Ireland. The Northern Ireland state consisted of six of the nine Ulster counties, the maximum deemed possible to assure a unionist majority in elections. The other 26 counties comprised the Southern Ireland state. Elections for the parliaments of both states were held in 1921 and the Northern Ireland parliament came into operation. Sinn Féin used the election for the Southern Ireland parliament as one for the second Dáil, and Sinn Féin candidates were returned unopposed in all constituencies. They included six women;

Markievicz, Margaret Pearse, mother of Patrick, Kathleen Clarke, Katherine O'Callaghan, Mary McSwiney and Dr Ada English.

In July 1921 a truce was agreed and was followed by negotiations. The heads of a Treaty, signed by the Irish delegation in December, gave the southern state full dominion status within the British Commonwealth of Nations, but not an independent republic. The Treaty was debated by the Dáil from December into January 1922, and accepted by a small majority. All six women deputies voted against it, Markievicz arguing that it would not deliver Connolly's aim of a socialist workers' republic.

During 1922 a committee worked on drafting the constitution for the new state. In June there was a general election intended to let the people judge the constitution. In the event the draft was published only on election day, and the central election issue was the Treaty itself. During the Dáil debates in March Katherine O'Callaghan proposed that the electorate be based on the local government electoral registers, thereby including more women than the limited 1918 franchise. From the records it appears that the proposal was supported by anti-Treaty deputies and opposed by pro-Treatyites, suggesting how deputies believed women were likely to vote, and it did not pass. The election returned 57 pro-Treaty and 46 anti-Treaty deputies. The Civil War began in June.

However the constitution of the Irish Free State which came into being in December 1922 gave full equality of citizenship to both sexes. Article 3 read:

> Every person, without distinction of sex, domiciled in the area of jurisdiction of the Irish Free State (Saorstát Éireann) ... who was born in Ireland ... shall ... enjoy the privileges and be subject to the obligations of such citizenship.

So, by 1922 feminists in the Irish Free State had succeeded in removing virtually all legal barriers to equality of citizenship. It remained to be seen how this would work out in practice.

The following decades saw a backlash against feminist gains in many countries. In the Free State Cumann na nGaedheal governments in the 1920s and Fianna Fáil governments in the 1930s clawed back different elements of equality. The 1924 and 1927 jury service acts resulted in women being removed from the basic register and having to apply to be put on it. The 1924 and 1926 civil service acts allowed discrimination on the basis of sex in competitive examinations for positions. 1932 legislation required female primary school teachers to retire on marriage. The criminal law amendment act of 1935 imposed fines and then imprisonment for soliciting by prostitutes while leaving clients untouched. The conditions of employment act of 1935 empowered the Minister for Labour to prohibit or limit the employment of women in industrial occupations.

Feminist organisation and resistance to the backlash continued throughout the decades, though smaller numbers were involved and the public profile lower. In the years from 1916 to 1922 nationalist feminists had inevitably been in the front line pressing feminist claims on the Sinn Féin male leadership. Now many prominent nationalist feminists, and the leadership of Cumann na mBan, rejected the Treaty, did not recognise the Free State and did not take part in its political structures, though many continued to be politically active in feminist and left-wing organisations. For several decades the few women TDs were elected on the basis of party affiliation, and there were no feminist voices in the Dáil. In the Seanad there were some, notably Jennie Wyse Power, Kathleen Clarke and Eileen Costello. Outside the Oireachtas feminist organisations were back in action, and vigorously opposed the regressive legislation. The IWSLGA, now with another change of name, the Irish Women Citizens and Local Government Association, and generally known as the Women Citizens, and the women graduate associations of both the National University and Dublin University were to the fore.

As before a broad range of issues continued to attract feminist action. The Joint Committee of Women's Societies and Social Workers was founded in 1935 to monitor social legislation affecting women and children and recommend reforms. It was composed of delegates from a wide range of organisations. Among the issues it campaigned for were women police; a 50 per cent representation of women in the new Seanad; amendments to the married women's maintenance act and the law on adoption; the substitution of boarding-out system for residential care for children in state care and appropriate training for social workers.

Several articles in the draft 1937 constitution were vigorously contested by feminists with varying results, and the idea of a women's political party emerged. In 1937 the Women's Social and Political League was formed to 'promote the political, social and economic status of women', and aimed to put forward independent women candidates for the Dáil, Seanad and public bodies. It changed 'political' to 'progressive' in 1938 to allow civil servants to join. During the general election of that year it campaigned on a range of issues: women's jury service, pay differentials between women and men in the various professions; the newly introduced enforced retirement of female primary school teachers at 60. In the 1943 general election it ran Hanna Sheehy Skeffington as its own candidate and backed three other women, all unsuccessfully.

In 1942 the Irish Housewives Association (IHA) was founded by a group of young middle-class married women in Dublin, on the initiative of Hilda Tweedy. Andrée Sheehy Skeffington, daugher-in-law of Hanna, was also a founding member. Their immediate objective was the equitable distribution of food and other scarce commodities during World War II. Their work and research led to the founding of the Consumers Association of Ireland. The IHA also had an explicit feminist outlook. It aimed to unite housewives 'to play an active part in all spheres of planning for the community' and 'a real equality of liberties, status and opportunity for all persons'. It took part in the campaign to elect Hanna Sheehy Skeffington. In 1947 the Women Citizens merged with the IHA, bringing with it a direct link to the founding of the Dublin Women's Suffrage Association in 1876, and an affiliation to the International Alliance of Women (IAW). This affiliation was actively maintained over the years, and Hilda Tweedy represented the IHA at IAW congresses from 1949 to 1986. It also led to the setting up of the first Commission on the Status of Women in 1970.

In 1967 the United Nations Commission on Women issued a directive to women's international organisations to instruct their affiliates to examine the status of women in their own country and, where necessary, urge their governments to set up national commissions. As a result the IHA and the Federation of Business and Professional Women's Clubs, established in 1965, jointly called a meeting of a wide range of women's organisations, and this set up a representative ad hoc committee. The committee identified issues needing action, including equal pay for equal work; discrimination against married women in employment and taxation, and girls' education. After a year's intensive lobbying, the Irish government set up the Commission on the Status of Women in 1970, with a remit to examine and report, make recommendations and indicate the implications – including the cost – of implementing them. The commission's report in 1972 made wide-ranging recommendations, including: the removal of discrimination based on sex or marriage in access to employment, pay, taxation, social security and pension schemes; better provision for deserted wives, unmarried mothers, widows, and wives of prisioners; equal liability for jury service; more women appointees to public bodies; co-education; and marriage-counselling and family-planning services. The women's organisations quickly established the Council for the Status of Women to ensure that the recommendations were implemented.

The 1960s was a decade of widespread challenges to establishments. Challenges included: the American Civil Rights movement; the Northern Ireland Civil Rights Association; student movements in many countries; the ecumenical movement; the Second Vatican Council and liberation theology in the Catholic Church; and the emergence of the second wave of the women's movement. Second-wave feminism arrived publicly on the Irish scene with the founding of the Irish Women's Liberation Movement (IWLM) in 1970. The new wave was larger than the first had ever been, had a higher public profile and was more widely diffused geographically and across class, religion and political affiliation. Consciousness-raising groups, based on the insight that 'the personal is political', tackled the internalised acceptance of current sex-role stereotypes that held many women back. The aim was a non-hierarchical mass movement that would sweep away all forms of gender discrimination.

At first the new wave saw the existing women's orgnisations as part of the establishment. Yet mutual recognition between the longer-established and the newer feminist groups developed quickly, and their cooperation during the 1970s helped to achieve a range of legislative reforms implementing many of the Commission's recommendations. The IWLM and its successor, the more left-wing Irish Women United (IWU), also contributed to the setting up of a range of services run by women for women, dealing with issues ranging from encouraging and fostering women's entry into public politics to family law, family planning, single parents' concerns, pregnancy issues, domestic violence, rape, and deserted wives and husbands. The feminist publishing houses, Arlen House (1975), Irish Feminist Information (1978), which became Attic Press (1984), and Women's Community Press (1983), were founded. In the general election of 1982 for the first time the established political parties ran candidates with a high profile in the women's movement. Gemma Hussey, Nuala Fennell and Monica Barnes were elected as Fine Gael TDs.

By the 1980s both the IWLM and IWU had disintegrated and there was no central organisation, yet the women's movement expanded and diversified. Women's studies emerged to develop research and analysis within and across the established disciplines, with the feminist publishers playing an important role. Women's studies expanded in a plethora of forms and locations from locally-based educational projects to university courses. They interacted with the emergence of women's groups in working-class communities, successors to the largely middle-class consciousness-raising groups of the 1970s. This was an important development as for the first time Irish working-class women in substantial numbers became active feminists, speaking and writing for themselves. Their feminism was generally one facet of the leadership role being taken by women in community activity generally, and particularly in the poorer housing estates.

Throughout the 1970s and 1980s the IHA was actively interested in and took part in many of the new directions of the women's movement. At the same time it maintained its active participation in the Council for the Status for Women, and in the International Alliance of Women. It also continued to campaign on consumer issues. By the 1990s it found it was not attracting enough new members to carry on its work effectively and decided to celebrate its contribution and dissolve on the occasion of its golden jubilee in 1992.

The IHA was a real and vital link in the long chain of the Irish women's movement. It carried on the original feminist project of gaining full and active citizenship for women. It broadened that by its work for consumers that aimed at fairer play contributing to the well-being of all sections of society. It continued and developed the participation of Irish feminism in the international movement. It always welcomed cooperation with other groups, and was in many ways a facilitating bridge between first and second wave feminism. It had its own unique direct link to the Dublin Women's Suffrage Assocation founded in 1876 at the beginning of organised feminism in Ireland. Through that link we have today the original minute book of the DWSA in the handwriting of Anna Haslam. Hilda Tweedy herself, with her energy, enthusiasm, wide interests and talent for friendship, was an inspirational link to many of us.

As the third wave of the women's movement develops it is important to ensure that it has available the history of the first and second waves. That will help it to understand how we have got to where we are, evaluate, learn from and dialogue with the first and second waves, assess where it agrees or disagrees with what it finds, and so be in a better position to decide on its future directions. Understanding Hilda Tweedy's life and work will be part of that history.

EQUALITY V. DIFFERENCE
THE CONSTRUCTION OF WOMANHOOD
IN MODERN IRISH FEMINIST THOUGHT

Maryann Gialanella Valiulis

One of the issues that has bedeviled modern feminist political theory is the equality/difference dilemma. Are women equal to or different from men? And, what are the implications of this dilemma for women's relationship to the State? Feminists throughout the modern Western world have grappled with this dilemma.[1] While Western male liberal political thought talked about inalienable rights and equality, women were, from the beginning, excluded from that discussion. Their difference from men – a difference that was usually situated in their reproductive capacities – seemed to take precedence over any contention of equality and appeared to preclude their participation in the public sphere, making women incapable of fulfilling political responsibilities.[2]

In fact, this emphasis on difference dictated that women have a dissimilar relationship to the State than men – an indirect relationship to the State. Women's association to the State was indirect because it was mediated by their connection to men – be they fathers, husbands, brothers or sons. Women's primary relationship, it was argued, was to the private sphere where their defining obligation was motherhood – an obligation which was often conceptualized in a broader framework to include nurturing and caring for children, husbands, elders. The important point was that it was these private, domestic responsibilities which took precedence over public rights and obligations.

This emphasis on difference spawned the idea of complementarity. Women, it was argued, had complementary attributes, talents and gifts – all of which suited them more to a domestic existence. Complementarity allowed theorists to skirt the issue of equality altogether or, while acknowledging the theoretical equality of women to men, emphasize the dichotomy upon which various dualities of dominance/subordination rested. For example, because of their so-called natural attributes, women belonged in the private sphere and should be homemakers and not venture into the public sphere.

The equality/difference dilemma has clearly vexed feminists who have argued for women's inclusion in the body politic – for the full rights and obligations of citizenship for women. Do women have the same inalienable rights as men? Should this be their justification for citizenship? Or should feminists stress difference, emphasizing the unique contributions that women make to the State as the basis for their citizenship? One feminist theorist has termed this 'the Wollstonecraft dilemma' – after the feminist theorist Mary Wollstonecraft – and has explained that:

> The dilemma arises because, within the existing patriarchal conception of citizenship, the choice always has to be made

between equality and difference, or between equality and womanhood. On the one hand, to demand 'equality' is to strive for equality with men (to call for the 'rights of men and citizens' to be extended to women), which means that women must become (like) men. On the other hand, to insist, like some contemporary feminists, that women's distinctive attributes, capacities and activities be revalued and treated as a contribution to citizenship is to demand the impossible; such difference is precisely what patriarchal citizenship excludes.[3]

Such a stark dilemma has not been in evidence in much of modern Irish political feminist discourse. Irish feminist discourse challenged patriarchal citizenship at its core. For the first half of the twentieth century it has dealt with the equality/difference issue by refusing to be constrained within the dichotomy. Instead, it has incorporated both elements within its discussion of women, especially within its discussion of women's relationship to the State. While modern Irish feminist discourse has chosen, at various times, to emphasize one or the other aspects of this duality, it has not fallen into the either/or trap. Instead it has opted for a discourse of inclusivity, depending on the particular historical context. This has given the idea of womanhood in Irish feminist discourse of the period a complex, dynamic and nuanced construction.

Irish feminists argued that women were indeed equal, but also had unique qualities to bring to the political sphere. Thus Irish feminist discourse incorporated both strands – equality and difference – and, in responding to particular circumstances, these feminists chose a political response which they believed would best achieve their goal of women's entry into the political sphere, of women's free and unfettered citizenship. In fact, in charting the emphasis of feminist discourse from the 1900s to mid century, what becomes clear is that what was important was the politics of location, the terrain in which they found themselves. Hence in times of political flux,

Irish feminists stressed their equality – a much more threatening argument – and in times of political repression, they emphasized their difference from men. Both were used to justify entrée onto the political stage. In none of these circumstances did they abandon their belief in both. But in each of the three periods examined here what is evident is that the politics of location, the political situation in which they were operating, influenced their emphasis on either equality or difference.

This article will examine three different periods in the evolution of the modern Irish State – the period of revolutionary fervour which preceded the foundation of the Irish Free State; the era of the founding of the Irish Free State; and the time of consolidation, the years following World War II – in terms of the feminist construction of womanhood. During these three periods, I will analyze some of the voices who challenged the dominant patriarchal attitude towards women's role in society and their relationship to the State and the way in which they cast their challenge. Specifically, I will focus on Inghinidhe na hÉireann, active at the turn of the century at the time when questions about the nature of the forthcoming Irish State were being hotly debated; the Irish feminists of the 1920s and 1930s, like the women in the Irish Women's Citizen and Local Government Association and the Irish Women's Equality League, who argued for full inclusion of women in the newly created State;[4] and the Irish Housewives Association, founded in 1942, who were claiming a public voice for women at a time of intense political conservatism. What emerges from analyzing the arguments, attitudes and activities of these feminists is that in their construction of womanhood, their emphasis on either equality or difference varied as the political system became more closed and hostile to women.

While the Irish political system may have varied in its degree of openness toward including women, Irish society's expectation for women did not alter significantly from the ninteenth century through to the 1960s. It was simply that of marriage and motherhood. Marriage and motherhood were seen as women's primary role in society and women's essential responsibility to society – a view which had the moral sanction of the Catholic Church and, with few exceptions, the political endorsement of politicians of various ideological backgrounds. Women who did not fit the model; those who worked outside the home, women who remained single, lesbian women, were all brushed aside in the dominant discourse of the period.

But there were voices which challenged this patriarchal discourse and expanded women's role beyond the home, beyond the private and into the public sphere. These were feminist voices which saw women not only as wives and mothers, but also as citizens in their own right, as political activists who had specific contributions to make to the political life of the State. Those feminists who were involved in carving out women's public space were a relatively small group of mostly urban women who were from the affluent classes, some well-educated, a few even holding university positions. In the earlier years, they were usually involved with the nationalist movement. Overall, they were politically prominent women whose stature and reputation gave them influence beyond their numbers.

One such group active at the turn of the century was Inghinidhe na hÉireann (The Daughters of Ireland). Specifically, I would like to concentrate on the feminist, nationalist ideology which they expressed through the pages of their newspaper, *Bean na hÉireann*. While there were certainly committed and articulate feminists who were not part of Inghinidhe na hÉireann – Hanna Sheehy Skeffington, for example – Inghinidhe na hÉireann is of note because it articulated a particular nationalist and feminist vision of the role of women in a free Ireland – a vision which feminists expected the new State to implement.

In the early years of the twentieth century, there was much debate about the nature of the forthcoming Irish State. It was a time of intellectual flux with ideas contesting with one another as intellectuals, political theorists and playwrights – nationalists of all varieties – tried to define the contours of the new state. Questions abounded, questions focusing on the conceptions of Irish identity which the new State would embody. How would Irishness be defined? How would an 'Irish' State – regardless of its political definition – be different than its English counterpart? What would the role of women be in the new State?

Inghinidhe na hÉireann entered into this debate. The women of Inghinidhe na hÉireann were a vibrant, self-confident group who challenged the status quo both in terms of nationalist and feminist ideology. Their importance lay not in terms of their numbers or even in terms of their actual activities. Their particular significance emerged from their ideology, from their attitude, from their stance in joining together militant nationalism and feminism. Indeed, it would be their particular contribution to challenge the traditional definition of a 'nationalist woman' by imagining a community in which feminism and nationalism neither conflicted nor competed, but rather co-existed in harmony. Their existence opened up new possibilities for women, new definitions for womanhood.

The Daughters of Ireland were relentless in demanding that women take their proper place in the nationalist movement of the day, in organizations such as Sinn Fein and the Gaelic League. Much can be said about Inghinidhe na hÉireann, but I would like to emphasize two of their key ideas. They believed that in a free Ireland, women should and would have political equality. They also believed that women needed to break free of the chains of domesticity.

In terms of the first theme, that in a free Ireland women should and would have political equality, the Daughters of Ireland believed that once Ireland was in control of its own destiny, women would play a prominent role in determining public policy.[5] In their newspaper, *Bean na hÉireann*, they proclaimed their belief that Irish men would treat Irish women fairly. Their expectations for political equality were high, believing it inconceivable that Irishmen would 'lower the standards of liberty' and continue to deny women their rights:

> The men of our race, descended like us, from a long line of martyrs in the cause of liberty, will not try to keep our rights and our duties from us, and the day that Ireland stands free before the world shall see our emancipation too.[6]

Bean na hÉireann had no doubt that not only would Irishwomen play a role in the new State, but that they had a right to participate in the public life of the country – in the struggle for independence, in political discussions, in policy decisions. To all who would listen, they proclaimed their belief in women's innate equality:

> Our desire to have a voice in directing the affairs of Ireland is not based on the failure of men to do so properly, but is the inherent right of women as loyal citizens and intelligent human souls.[7]

In addition to emphasizing equality, *Bean na hÉireann* also believed that women would contribute something different, something unique to political life by their participation:

> It is not our intention to countenance any sex antagonism between Irish women and Irish men ... but we think that men

would be the better for a little of women's unselfishness and
spirituality, and we look for the advent of women into public
life for a lofty idealism and a purer atmosphere.[8]

They argued that because women were different from
men, had different qualities, there were clear advantages
which would accrue to the forthcoming State if women
participated in the political life of the country. Moreover,
the Daughters of Ireland were confident that women's role
in the new State would incorporate more than simply a
domestic identity. Indeed, they argued that women
needed to break free of the chains of domesticity. The
columns of *Bean na hÉireann* increasingly rejected the idea
that women should be confined to the domestic sphere. In
fact, they explicitly took issue with the notion of separate
spheres for men and women. For example, on the tenth
anniversary of the founding of Inghinidhe na hÉireann,
Bean na hÉireann proclaimed that the Daughters' work
'exploded forever that silly "women's sphere" idea, which
always stifles the high courage and patriotism which is in
every Irishwoman's heart'.[9] It was, the newspaper
proclaimed, to the credit of Inghinidhe na hÉireann that
they destroyed the idea that 'the sphere of women is
bounded by frying pans and fashion plates'.[10]

What *Bean na hÉireann* was saying was that domesticity
was boring, domesticity was stifling. Domesticity did
nothing to further either women's growth and
development or the freedom of Ireland. What was needed
was comradeship and full citizenship:

> ... It is only by the frank admission of women into the equal
> rights of citizenship with men that we can hope for a further
> advance in domestic life.[11]

This rejection of the idea of separate spheres, of the
domestic realm as women's natural habitat, and
Inghinidhe na hÉireann's insistence on women's right to
be considered as citizens is important in establishing an

alternative model of womanhood for nationalist feminist women. The Daughters of Ireland thus delineated a wider definition of what was appropriate for women, more than that, what it was women's obligation to do for the nationalist movement. Their gender ideology expanded women's role into the public sphere where women would work as partners with men in the broader political scene. In an intellectually radical period, Inghinidhe na hÉireann expressed that radicalism in a feminist vision of woman as citizen.

This vision of woman as citizen contrasted dramatically with the stark reality of independence. During the initial years of independence, rather than acknowledge women's right to a place in the political realm, successive governments sought to re-establish, with a high degree of rigidity, the doctrine of separate spheres, to define women out of politics.

In fact, simply put, the first governments of the Irish Free State sought to eliminate women from public life. Although the Constitution of 1921 gave women over the age of 21 the right to vote and hold office on terms of equality with men, that formal equality was undermined by the government's subsequent gender legislation:

1) The Juries Acts of 1924 and 1927 which, for all practical purpose, barred women from serving on juries;

2) The 1925 Civil Service Act which restricted women's right to employment at all levels in the Civil Service;

3) the 1932 ban on employing married women teachers, a ban which eventually applied to the entire civil service;

4) the 1935 Employment Act which gave the Minister for Industry and Commerce the right to restrict the number of women employed in any given industry;

5) Finally, the 1937 Constitution which explicitly assigned women the role of guardians of the hearth and family.

Taken together, this legislation represents nothing less than an attack on women's citizenship and women's claim to a rightful space in the public sphere. Moreover, it should be noted that these were rights which women already had and which Irish governments chose to take away from them. Thus, the situation is not that women were agitating to gain more rights – unlike, for example, the situation in the US in the 1920s where feminists were agitating for the right to serve on juries. In the Irish Free State, successive governments had to take specific action to introduce legislation which took away rights which women already possessed and which severely limited women's political and economic freedom. The governments of the Irish Free State defined women out of the public realm. Successive governments sent women a very clear message – they were to be restricted to the domestic sphere, to be rendered publicly invisible.

This restricted definition of Irish womanhood was based on two main assumptions. In the first place, the dominant discourse asserted that the primary role of women was marriage and motherhood. What this meant was that woman's place was in the home tending to the needs of their husbands and children, with the corollary that true Irish women recognized and embraced this fact. True Irish women, said the government and its supporters, had no desire to be wrenched from 'the bosoms of their families, from their cherished household duties, from the preparation of their husband's dinners'.[12] Only those who were not normal – to use the words of the Minister for Justice – wished to take part in the public life of the country. Invoking the concept of abnormal during the 1920s and juxtaposing it with words like monstrous and repugnant – which the dominant political discourse did quite regularly – can be seen to have as its subtext the charge of lesbianism. It is precisely in this period that lesbianism is identified and defined as an abnormality.

Clearly, this type of attack was meant to discredit feminists and all those who challenged the dominant male political elite.

The second premise of the government and of the dominant patriarchal discourse was that women were not necessary to the public life of the country. Interestingly, in this argument, the government reversed the 'difference' argument which feminists had made about women contributing something unique, something different to the public sphere. The government maintained that women were really the same as men, that they were not necessary to the public life of the country, that indeed the public life would flow more smoothly and more efficiently without women. Women, they argued, simply encumbered the process and wasted time and money. Interestingly, the government did not use 'same' to mean equal. It just meant that women had no extra value to bring to the political system.

More than that, the government claimed that women brought chaos and confusion to the normal operation of the public sphere. In the instance of women serving on juries, for example, special facilities would be required which would disrupt the normal flow of the system. It was not a new argument. This association of women with chaos and disorder has long historical roots in patriarchal thinking, going back at least to the Old Testament and the sin of Eve. In sum, the government argued that women had nothing special to contribute, were not necessary and indeed were agents of chaos and disorder.

Not surprisingly, Irish feminists of the 1920s and 1930s rejected – often with passion, sometimes with stinging sarcasm – the government's definition of them and its restricted definition of Irish womanhood. They countered with a much broader, more inclusive position which asserted women's equality as well as women's difference.

It also questioned the belief that there was an unbridgeable gap between the public and private sphere.

In terms of the equality argument, feminists claimed that women were equal under the law and hence had a right to political and economic equality. It was a straightforward argument. The right to equality, they argued, was guaranteed to them under the 1922 Constitution which granted women full citizenship. As equals, women should have both the rights and privileges of citizenship as well as the corresponding responsibilities and obligations. Like Inghinidhe na hÉireann, they spoke of the woman citizen.

However, feminists of the 1920s and 1930s also added a new dimension to the equality argument by adding to the concept of legal equality the idea of practical or participatory equality. Feminists pointed out quite bluntly that they had earned full citizenship and inclusion in the body politic on terms of equality with men by their participation in the revolutionary struggle.[13] Women had given a practical demonstration of their worth as citizens when the very existence of the state was an issue. Senator Jennie Wyse Power eloquently made this point in the Senate during the Civil Service Amendment Act:

> No men in a fight for freedom ever had such loyal cooperation from their women as the men who compose the present Executive Council. When they wanted messengers to go into dangerous places, they did not call on members of their own sex. When they wanted auditors to go out when the old Local Government Board broke down it was women they sent. It was women inspectors that went round ... and did all the work for them in that terrible time and these are the people who tell us that we are physically unfit. I regret that this has come from the men who were associated in the fight with women who played their part at a time when sex and money were not considerations.[14]

This argument is reminiscent of the ideas found on the pages of *Bean na hÉireann* wherein the Daughters of Ireland spoke of the common shouldering of burdens, of women as comrades. On those pages, however, feminists argued that their participation in the revolutionary struggle would be proof, to the very few who might need it, of women's equality. They certainly did not anticipate the situation which prevailed in the Irish Free State.

In addition to asserting equality, feminist discourse of the 1920s and 1930s flatly contradicted the government's position that women were not necessary in the public sphere and argued that indeed women's presence in public life would confer distinctive benefits on the system.

Using society's view that women's 'natural role' was motherhood, feminist discourse argued that, arising out of that role, women had something unique, something different from men to contribute. Because of their role as child-rearers and nurturers, feminists asserted that women had insights denied to men, insights which made their presence in the public life of the state mandatory. This directly countered the government's argument that women brought nothing to the public sphere which would justify the expense and disorder which their presence created.

Feminist discourse of the 1920s and 1930s also took issue with the idea that women, because of their responsibilities in the private sphere, should be restricted to that arena. This argument called into question the division between the public and private sphere and directly challenged those who wished to maintain an insurmountable barrier between the two. Women, they argued, despite the claims of the private sphere, could also fulfill a role in the public sphere. Moreover, feminists asserted that not only were women entitled to a space in the public arena, but that because of their unique contributions, it was necessary for them to cross over into the public sphere.

These feminists argued that marriage and family did not preclude public participation. This idea, they claimed, was simply an argument used against any type of 'progress' which was made to keep them in the home. As one woman noted:

> It is extraordinary how the poor, dinnerless husband manages to survive in this country as an argument against almost any kind of progress. In pre-war days it was the Parliamentary franchise. If a woman left her home for the period of time necessary to record her vote it might entail the dread possibility of her husband's having no dinner (masculine imagination apparently could picture no greater calamity).[15]

Irish feminists thus uncovered one underlying motive for men's insistence on the rigid separation of private and public. Women performed, in the male view, necessary domestic activities such as cooking dinners – an example which surfaces numerous times in male political discourse of the period – allowing men to concentrate totally and completely on the public sphere. Women's participation in the public sphere had the potential to disrupt those activities, to bring 'chaos and disorder' to the rigid separation which men had maintained. Equally important, feminist discourse raised uncomfortable questions about the necessity of keeping those two spheres separated.

Thus the feminists of the 1920s and 1930s sought to reclaim their rights and responsibilities as citizens. They rejected the equality v. difference dichotomy, refusing to be restricted to one or the other. They argued that yes, women were equal. They also argued that yes, women were different. And, they argued that both together made women invaluable citizens. By bringing together both the equal rights and difference arguments, feminists created a counter definition of women's citizenship.[16]

The arguments of the feminists of the 1920s and 1930s reflected the political climate which they confronted. The reality of independence was far different from that which Inghinidhe na hÉireann had envisioned. The Irish Free State was a much more conservative site than many of those involved in the revolutionary period would have anticipated. In 1922, even those who might have been considered 'revolutionary' were of the more conservative branch. One needs only to think of Kevin O'Higgins' comment that he and his colleagues in government were among the most conservative revolutionaries who ever lived. The radicalism of 1916 was difficult to find in 1922.

Feminists had to adapt to this changing climate and their discourse reflected the conservatism of the Free State. They were not saying that domesticity is boring, or that they chose to be comrades, not wives as did Inghinidhe na hÉireann. Rather feminists of the 1920s and 1930s took on the identity of motherhood, nurturer and care-giver and used it as a justification for participation in the body politic. Rather than mounting a direct challenge to the dominant male discourse of the period, they subverted the discourse for their own purposes and argued for both equality and difference. The next generation of feminists would use this same tactic, but would increasingly emphasize women's experience in the private sphere, would highlight women's difference as a justification of for women's inclusion in the public sphere.

As it matured, the Irish Free State became increasingly conservative and more rigid in its delineation of gender roles and its insistence on the separation of the private and public spheres. The marriage bar prevented many married women from working outside the home, lack of contraception meant that women had no control of the size of their families, and an economy which was less than robust provided little leeway for women to break through gender barriers which seemed to be firmly entrenched. Women in public life became an increasingly rare species. Feminists were left with little room to manoeuvre.

Despite the conservative climate, there was a new group of feminists who were determined to play their part in the political life of the State. With the founding of the Irish Housewives Association (IHA) in 1942, another generation of activists came to the fore with, however, a perceptible shift in the emphasis of feminist thought. Interestingly and significantly, when Hilda Tweedy and Andrée Sheehy Skeffington approached Hanna Sheehy Skeffington about founding the new organization and its new name, they were met with the reproach 'You are not married to the house you know'.[17] As the historian Margaret Ward points out, Hanna 'could not bear the name "housewife" and, in truth, the name gave a misleading impression of the kind of woman who joined'.[18]

The name, however, reflected the reality for many Irish women. It fused together the seeming opposite identities of housewife and citizen, the seeming opposite spheres of public and private. It used women's role in the home as a justification for their involvement in the public sphere. For the Irish Housewives Association, it was not a question of women being housewives and also citizens as if they were separate and distinct identities. But rather its discourse grounded women's obligation to participate in the public sphere in her role as homemaker in the private sphere. It brought together personal and political identities. As Hilda Tweedy wrote on the occasion of the Silver Jubilee Issue of *The Irish Housewife*: 'We were the housekeepers in our own home and we felt we should utilize our talents and experience in the national housekeeping'.[19]

This fusion represented a shift in emphasis from the feminist discourse of the 1920s and 1930s who argued that women were citizens of the public sphere and nurturers of the private sphere, noting that their work in the latter gave them insights denied to men. The Irish Housewives Association pushed this idea of difference one step further. They explicitly used the knowledge which women acquired in the home, their work in the home, as a justification for their participation in the public sphere. It was an argument which seemed to move beyond the women as citizen and housewife to housewife as citizen.

The Irish Housewives Association began as a pressure group to improve living conditions in an Ireland dealing with war-time shortages, but continued and expanded their work well into the post-war period. Its first two basic aims reveal much about its character:

1) To unite housewives so that they shall recognize, and gain recognition for, their right to play an active part in all spheres of planning for the community;

2) to secure all such reforms as are necessary to establish a real equality of liberties, status and opportunity for all persons.

The next two aims went on to discuss the rights of consumers.[20] The IHA thus demanded a public role for women and the right of the people of Ireland, especially and primarily the women of Ireland, to influence public policy.

While its name seemed to belie a feminist orientation, it was feminist in its emphasis on women, in its demands for equality, for a voice for women in the public sphere, for recognition of the work that women did, and in its attempt to improve the status of women. As Hilda Tweedy has pointed out:

The Irish Housewives always had an interest in feminist issues. We learned that making pleas to the government was not enough. We needed committed women in political life, women in the places where the decisions were being made.[21]

The IHA was feminist, political and grounded explicitly in the home.

The formation of the Irish Housewives Association reflected a recognition on the part of its founders that an organization which valued the role of housewife and which used it as a springboard for political activity and consciousness-raising had a higher chance of success than a National Woman's Party – the abandoned dream of Hanna Sheehy Skeffington. It publicly proclaimed its belief that women were badly needed in public life, because, as one member noted, men had been revealed as being incompetent – 'man's maladroitness' – in dealing with certain 'simple problems'.[22] The IHA, therefore, argued that women should help formulate at least those policies which had a direct impact on families, on the domestic economy:

> ... that only women, particularly housewives, had the understanding and experience to deal with the many problems which affect the running of a home, or the rearing of a family, and that they should claim their right in view of this experience, to have a say in the national housekeeping and home-making; to decide, for example, which we need most, imports of nylon stockings, exotic perfumes and foreign wines, or essential foodstuffs and raw material for our own industries.[23]

The Irish Housewives Association clearly believed that women were competent and well-able to make those important decisions. It was appalled that 'matters of great domestic interest are solidly in the hands of men. Strange as it may seem, there is not a woman in the Ministry of Supplies'.[24]

One of the strengths of the Irish Housewives Association was its valuing of the Irish housewife and the everyday knowledge which housewives accumulated in the home. The IHA invested the role of housewife with a practical dignity. It claimed for them a clearly defined position in the formulation of public policy, and a right to:

take our place with confidence in the front ranks of the Nation's builders for the future – not as a menial but as an honoured partner ... By singly and in groups, asking for and being determined to get, what is our right as consumers and citizens, we will make ourselves felt as an important factor in the life of the country.[25]

Thus members of the Irish Housewives Association petitioned ministers, monitored the distribution and pricing of goods and demanded policy changes in Emergency and post-war Ireland.

The Irish Housewives Association continued the tradition of feminist discourse in demanding a role for women in the public sphere, in the political life of the country. The Irish Housewives Association also continued the tradition used by feminists in the 1920s and 1930s of not challenging the dominant discourse, but rather using it as a basis for political action, of creating a political identity for women premised on domesticity. In the analysis of one observer, they were stretching the term housewife to expand beyond the private into the public sphere, to take on a public identity not simply a private one. Rather than reject this private identity, they defined it in a broader, more inclusive manner.[26] Invoking the doctrine of maternalism, the Irish Housewives Association, in ways reminiscent of the feminists of the 1920s and 1930s, asserted their moral authority based on their position in the home, and, as in other countries at other times, found 'powerful justification for the emergence of women from the home into the widened sphere of public work'.[27]

What becomes apparent from this analysis is the flexibility of feminist discourse in the first half of the century to adapt to the political context in which it was operating. In the early years of the twentieth century, the political climate was fluid – dreams and visions filled the air. Inghinidhe na hÉireann was part of that ferment, their discourse was radical, visionary. The feminists of the 1920s and 1930s were dealing with the reality of independence, when the State was defining itself, taking on its character. These feminists fought for women's rights within the context of an increasingly conservative State – much less fluid, much less open to negotiation, but still in the process of defining itself. The Irish Housewives Association were part of a State that had consolidated itself, had defined itself as Catholic, conservative, traditional, almost rigid. Within this context, they created a public space for women.

Despite this adaptability, there was a certain consistency to feminist discourse in this period. All of them believed uncompromisingly in women's political equality, an equality which conferred on women the rights and responsibilities of citizenship. This was the constant, unchanging note among all three groups.

However, this definition of equality did not mean sameness. Feminists were not arguing that women were the same as men. Rejecting sameness, therefore, allowed them, in varying degrees, to embrace women's difference, to argue that women had something unique, something different to bring to the public life of the state.

An analysis of the feminist discourse of all three groups also reveals the common demand that women be given a formal role in the public sphere, and a desire to overcome the false dichotomy of public and private, to renegotiate women's relationship to the state. This is important because, as noted above, women traditionally had a relationship to the state that was derivative, indirect. Women's civic identity was subsumed under that of the dominant male in their lives – fathers, husbands, brothers. Feminists sought to change this indirect relationship. The quest for the ballot, for suffrage, the demand to sit on juries, to have more women elected to the Dáil, to have women influence policy, to serve in the government were all a repudiation of the indirect relationship of women to the State and an endorsement of the individual civic identity of women, of the right of women to a direct relationship to the State.

Feminist discourse, especially later feminist discourse, also undermined the public/private split. By grounding their rationale for women's participation in the public sphere in her activities in the private sphere, they eroded this artificial division. Feminists proclaimed that woman as citizen was not incongruous with woman as housewife and homemaker. Indeed they used it as a reason why women must, therefore, have a role in the public affairs of the State. Making common cause with first wave feminists in countries such as the US and England, these Irish women, 'transformed a misogynistic discourse about differences between the sexes into an alternative discourse about female uniqueness designed to advance women's status and opportunities'.[28]

Feminists throughout the first half of the century gave voice to a perspective, a point of view which was woman-centered. They did not give up the quest for a role in the public life of the country. In all sorts of ways women kept up the demand for a place in the political process. They continued to sit on County Councils. They ran for public office. They protested infringements of their rights. They agitated for a more equitable and better quality of life for all.

Modern Irish feminist discourse has proven itself immensely resilient in negotiating the equality/difference dichotomy. It constructed a model of womanhood which encompassed both equality and difference. By refusing to be limited to a static, single dimensional view which saw woman either as political actor or as homemaker, feminists argued for a more complex, more dynamic model of womanhood. Feminist discourse – be it in the columns of *Bean na hÉireann*, or the letters of the feminists of the 1920s and 1930s, or in the columns of the *The Irish Housewife*, left an ideal which did not deny either women's public or private identity. It astutely embraced both.

NOTES

1   See, for example, Joan Scott's discussion of this debate in the French context or the debate in England in the postwar period between Eleanor Rathbone and the Six Point feminists.

2   See, for example, Carole Pateman's work on this topic, especially, *The Disorder of Women: Democracy, Feminism and Political Theory* (Stanford, Stanford University Press, 1989).

3   Carole Pateman, 'Equality, difference, subordination: the politics of motherhood and women's citizenship', in Gisela Bock and Susan James (eds), *Beyond Equality and Difference* (London, Routledge, 1992), p. 20.

4   There were many feminists groups in Ireland during this period – the Women's Graduate Association, the Irish Women's Citizen and Local Government Association and Irish Women's Equality League. In addition, there were numerous women's groups like the Irish Women Workers' Union, the Irish Countrywomen's Association. The names of the women involved in these organizations – thanks to women's history – are now familiar to us: Hanna Sheehy Skeffington, Maud Gonne, Con Markievicz, Mary Kettle, Mary Hayden, Jennie Wyse Power, Helena Moloney, Louie Bennett, as well as numerous others. Obviously this list of organizations and names is not exhaustive. It is rather a sampling of the many and varied women's groups which have dotted the landscape during this period.

5   There were, of course, dissenting voices which argued that Irish women had to insure their political identity by obtaining the vote. Hanna Sheehy Skeffington, for example, wrote extensively on this theme. Suffragists insisted that women had a right to the vote, even if it meant petitioning an English Parliament. Nationalist women, on the other hand, insisted

that women had to work for the freedom of Ireland to insure women's rights. For a discussion of this conflict, see *Bean na hÉireann*. Among the secondary works which deal with this issue, see Charlotte Fallen, *Soul of Fire: A Biography of Mary MacSwiney* (Cork, Mercier Press, 1986); Leah Levenson and Jerry Naderstad, *Hanna Sheehy Skeffington: A Pioneering Irish Feminist* (New York, Syracuse University Press, 1986); Beth McKillen, 'Irish Feminism and National Separatism, 1914–1923', *Eire Ireland* (Fall 1981 and Winter 1982); Marie O'Neill, *From Parnell to De Valera: A Biography of Jennie Wyse Power* (Dublin, Blackwater Press, 1991); Rosemary Cullen Owens, *Smashing Times* (Dublin, Attic Press, 1984); and Margaret Ward, *Unmanageable Revolutionaries; Women and Irish Nationalism* (Dingle, Co. Kerry, Brandon Books, 1983).

6   *Bean na hÉireann*, Vol. 1, No. 3, January, 1909.

7   *Bean na hÉireann*, Vol. 1, No. 3, January, 1909, Editorial.

8   *Bean na hÉireann*, Vol. 1, No. 3, January, 1909, Editorial.

9   *Bean na hÉireann*, No. 20, n.y., Editorial Notes.

10 *Bean na hÉireann*, No. 20, n.y., Editorial Notes.

11 *Bean na hÉireann*, Vol. 1, No. 3, January, 1909, Editorial reply.

12 Editorial in the *Dundalk Democrat* quoted in the *Irish Independent*, 14 February 1927. See also, for example, articles in the *Kilkenny People* and the *Evening Herald*. These newspapers were highly critical of women who wished to serve on juries.

13 This is not an uncommon occurrence. For example, African-Americans who fought in World War II against the despotic regimes of Nazism and Fascism returned home after the war and claimed their rights to a democracy they had fought for.

14 *Senate Debates* (Senator Wyse Power), Vol. 6, 17 December 1925, col. 258–259.

15 Letter to the Editor, *Irish Times*, 17 February 1927.

16 Ann Taylor Allen, 'Maternalism in German Feminist Movements', *Journal of Women's History*, Vol. 5, No. 2 (Fall 1993), p. 101. Allen argues that, in the German context, the synthesis of equal-rights and maternalist arguments created a 'new vision of women's citizenship in a state transformed by the infusion of female energies, skills, and values'.

17 Margaret Ward, *Hanna Sheehy Skeffington* (Cork, Attic Press, 1997), p. 338.

18 *Ibid.*

19   Hilda Tweedy, 'Looking Back', *The Irish Housewife*, Silver Jubilee Issue, 1966/1967, p. 15.

20   Hilda Tweedy, *A Link in the Chain* (Dublin, Attic Press, 1992), p. 18.

21   *Ibid*.

22   Petronella O'Flanagan, 'Woman and Scapegoat', *The Irish Housewives Association Yearbook*, 1950, Vol. 4, pp 13–14. Interestingly, the article also makes reference to the fact that women's participation in the public sphere, 'the emancipation of women' has not meant that women have neglected men or that men have been left to cook their own meals – another reference to the concern about 'dinnerless husbands' mentioned in 1927.

23   Hilda Tweedy, 'Housewives …', *The Irish Housewives Association Yearbook*, 1948, p. 9.

24   Susan Manning, 'Foreward', *The Irish Housewives Association Yearbook*, 1946, Vol. 1, p. 7.

25   'Foreward', *The Irish Housewives Association Yearbook*, 1948, p. 7.

26   Amanda Lagerkvist, 'To End Woman's Night', *Irish Journal of Feminist Studies*, Vol. 2, No. 2 (Winter, 1997), p. 29. Article pp 18–33.

27   Ann Taylor Alien, 'Maternalism in German Feminist Movements', *Journal of Women's History*, Vol. 5, No. 2 (Fall, 1993), p. 100.

28   Linda Gordon, 'On Difference', *Genders*, Vol. 10 (Spring, 1991), p. 91.

WOMEN IN IRELAND IN THE 1930S AND 1940S

Caitríona Clear

On the face of it women in newly independent Ireland were in an enviable position. Full political equality with men was guaranteed by the Free State Constitution of 1922 and women were not barred from any educational institutions or occupations. There were women writers, broadcasters, journalists, artists and actresses on stage and screen, and female veterans of the national struggle were held in high regard. Women sat in both houses of the Oireachtas and were eligible for the highest political offices in the land. However, apparent equality and occasional visibility masked long-standing problems of female unemployment and underemployment, and low levels of female organization throughout the country.

The unrelenting attacks on women's citizenship and employment rights have been well-documented – exemption from jury duty in 1927, the marriage bar against National teachers and other public servants from the early 1930s, the employment legislation of the mid-1930s and the apparent equation of women with domesticity alone in the

Constitution of 1937.[1] These attacks did not originate in any coherent anti-feminist ideology on the part of policy-makers. Unlike in Britain and Germany, women in Ireland were simply not numerous enough in paid work or public life to be resented or feared. They were simply collateral damage in economic policies designed to boost male employment. Female voices raised in protest were so easily ignored and dismissed that they didn't even have to be silenced.[2]

The 1930s and 1940s, however, were decades of inexorable, if slow, change for Irish girls and women. In 1936, two kinds of traditional work for women remained strong, the one, unpaid – assisting relative in agriculture – and the other, underpaid – domestic service. Women in these categories made up over half – 54% – of females gainfully occupied, i.e. working in Ireland in this year. Ten years later in 1946, 47.7% of all working women fell into these categories. Although not a very dramatic fall, this was an irreversible one, which accelerated in the late 1940s and 1950s. The occupational and social landscape of Ireland was in a state of transformation. Women workers were not only leaving the land, they were also leaving the houses of other women. Right into the 1950s Irish women's permanent rejection of domestic service was imagined to be temporary by middle-class employers (among them some members of the Irish Housewives Association and some members of government commissions) in a state of shocked denial.[3] But Irish girls and women were unstoppably on the move.

And where were they going? There were 4,000 more women in industrial work in Ireland in 1936 than there had been ten years earlier, and 8,000 more women in white-collar, clerical and administrative work. Numbers of women in industry fell slightly between 1936 and 1946, but even this depressed decennial period saw an additional

7,000 women making it into white-collar work. Lest this picture shine too brightly, however, we should note that these two categories, taken along with the two other common, non-domestic occupations for women, shop service and the professions (mainly teaching and nursing), while they made up 37% of the female workforce in 1946, still made up only 11.5% of the total adult female population in that year.[4] The gate to 'modern' non-domestic waged or salaried work was extremely narrow. The ports, on the other hand, were wide open, and girls and women made up at least half of all emigrants to Britain between 1940 and 1960.[5]

Emigration was a rational response by many girls and women to the shortage of well-paid and interesting work at home. Professional training which usually had to be paid for in Ireland – nursing – was a paying proposition in the large teaching hospitals of Britain, whose beguiling advertisements promising every facility, from on-site hairdressers to Roman Catholic chapels, featured weekly in Irish newspapers and magazines well into the 1950s.[6]

Late marriage (or no marriage at all) was an equally rational response by women to their economic situation. Marriage bars against National teachers and other public servants, to say nothing of the informal marriage bars operating in private companies and offices, had the undoubted result of postponing marriage for many women who were so inclined. Indeed, it was partly because of this that the marriage bar on female National teachers was lifted in 1958.[7] Deferred marriage is often regarded as a demographic and social tragedy, but it had (and arguably still has) advantages for women. They embark upon married life with some money saved, perhaps some authority gained from working life, and often a circle of friends and acquaintances. A shorter child-bearing period for the woman who married at 29 instead of 24, meant a comparatively smaller, more manageable family – no small consideration at a time when birth control was not only unavailable, but unthinkable for many women. Some women decided not to marry at all, so as to hold on to their jobs and their independence. It became a commonplace in the 1950s to blame low marriage rates on irresponsible 'eternal bachelors',[8] but the real obstacle to early and near-universal marriage wasn't the man who refused to settle down, but the woman who refused to settle for a poor standard of living.

Another feature adding to the discontent of women in particular in Ireland in these decades was the feeling that they were lagging behind the rest of the world as far as the material quality of life was concerned. In the 1940s in particular, Irish-produced magazines and women's pages in newspapers, to say nothing of household advice literature, all took the serviced (i.e. with piped water and electricity, or at least gas) suburban house as the norm, both in advertising and in editorial copy. However, basic standards of accommodation for working-class people in Ireland were rising from the early 1930s, when a massive building programme provided water on tap and light and cooking by switch for tens of thousands of families countrywide. Kileely, St Mary's Park, Bohermore, Gurranebraher, Drimnagh were heaven for women of the house who no longer had to change bedroom into living-room and back again twice a day, or lug clean and dirty buckets up and down stairs, or hang laundry precariously out of upper windows, or keep up an all-day-every-day battle against vermin, damp and smells. Tenements, lanes and courts were seen more and more in the 1930s and 1940s as a standing reproach to the government and society. Maura Laverty believed that her novel *Lift Up Your Gates* (1946) was banned because of its graphic description of the discomforts and dangers of tenement life.[9] Significantly, her fictional Liffey Lane is about to be pulled down and its inhabitants moved out to a new estate when the action of the novel takes place.

Out the country, electrification and aquafication didn't become universal till the 1960s, even early 1970s, and in the 1930s and 1940s most country houses on all size farms and most labourers' dwellings were without piped water and electricity. While this undoubtedly involved hardship of the 'pulling and dragging' variety, it did not give rise to chronic ill-health and high mortality. Waste could be dealt with efficiently and ergonomically, water for drinking was clean, pure milk was easily accessible, and diet for country people of all social classes was more nutritious than that of most urban dwellers, according to the National Nutrition Survey of the late 1940s.[10] Rural area always had much lower rates of infant mortality (i.e. babies dying in their first year or so of life) than urban areas.[11]

Infant and maternal mortality, those two infallible markers of public health and wellbeing, were, nonetheless, quite high in independent Ireland in the 1930s and 1940s, and they weren't much better in Northern Ireland.[12] The introduction of children's allowances in the Republic in 1944, though initially payable to fathers rather than mothers, had a discernible effect on women's health, and various public health initiatives of the late 1940s culminating in the implementation of a pared down version of Noel Browne's Mother and Child provisions in 1953, saw the inexorable decline in the number of women dying in childbirth by the mid-1950s. Infant mortality fell in the succeeding decade.[13] But in the 1930s and 1940s having a baby was still a precarious business, particularly for poor and malnourished women. Families were large, and Irish obstetricians developed world-class specialist expertise in the problems of the 'grande multipara', the woman who had given birth to five or more full-term infants.[14] Advising their patients to prevent pregnancy by any means other than abstinence was something doctors dared not do, even had they believed, as many did not, that such advice was right.[15] Books on Catholic medical theology discussed in detail when and under what circumstances it was morally permissible for couples to delay or space births, even by 'natural' means.[16] Maternal ill-health was bad enough, but maternal death, all too preventable, was a tragic end for the woman herself and a catastrophe for any children she already had. Her maternal role could only be filled by a daughter or sister who often gave up her own chances of work, training and even marriage. Irish women's magazines' problem pages in the 1950s and 1960s regularly featured the frustration of these women when the younger generation was reared and they had no job, no marriage and no prospect of either.[17]

The Irish Housewives Association was founded at a time when the word 'housewife' was not in common use among Irish women – disliked by many, it was coming to be accepted only very slowly twenty years later.[18] However the IHA's concerns – women and consumer affairs, women's health and welfare – were central to the 54% or so of the female population who were described by the census in 1946 as 'engaged in home duties'.[19] This category included farmers' wives, most of whom did as much farm work as housework, and many of whom commanded and controlled sums of money from poultry and dairying. It included shopkeepers' and artisans' wives who ran the business jointly in all but name, doing the accounts and dealing with customers and clients. It included women with their families reared, widows, and married women who had never had children. It also, in the 1930s and 1940s, included a sizeable proportion of single women (over a fifth of all women engaged in home duties were single in these decades, 22% in 1936, 21% in 1946), keeping house for adult or younger siblings, or looking after aged parents.[20] Whoever they were and whatever their circumstances, the IHA's concerns about prices and quality of goods were increasingly relevant to them, as more and more household requirements were being bought at shops, rather than grown, made or reared at home. However, the 1930s and 1940s were also characterized quite strongly by the determination of a growing number of Irish women never to have the designation 'housewife', or at least, to postpone it until they had exhausted the possibilities of other more remunerative identities.

NOTES

1   Mary Clancy, 'Aspects of Women's Contribution to Oireachtas Debate in Ireland 1922–37', in Cliona Murphy and Maria Luddy (eds), *Women Surviving* (Dublin, Poolbeg, 1990), pp 206–32; Caitríona Clear, *Women of the House: Women's Household Work in Ireland, 1922–61* (Dublin, Irish Academic Press, 2000), pp 27–67; Caitriona Beaumont, 'After the Vote: Women, Citizenship and the Campaign for Gender Equality in the Irish Free State 1922–43', in Louise Ryan and Margaret Ward (eds), *Irish Women and the Vote: Becoming Citizens* (Dublin, Irish Academic Press, 2007), pp 231–49. See also Yvonne Scannell, 'The Constitution and the Role of Women', in Brian Farrell (ed.), *De Valera's Constitution and Ours* (Dublin, Gill and Macmillan, 1988), pp 123–36.

2   A good summary of European countries in the interwar period can be found in Gisela Bock and Pat Thane (eds), *Maternity and Gender Policies: Women and the Rise of European Welfare States 1880s–1950s* (London, Routledge, 1991), especially contributions by the two editors on the two countries in question.

3   All the figures here are taken from the analysis of occupational tables in decennial censuses as presented and discussed in Clear, *House.*, pp 1–26. On domestic servants and the Irish Housewives Association, see the optimistic and upbeat tone of Elizabeth Boyle, 'A Plan for the Northern Houseworkers', *The Irish Housewife*, Vol. 1 (1946), pp 31–3, and 'Joan', 'The Home Front', *ibid.*, Vol. 4 (1950), pp 103–5. The realization that domestic servants had gone for good, never to return, had dawned by 1956 when W. Letts penned 'Bracing Thoughts on a Universal

Duty', *Ibid.*, Vol. 9 (1956), pp 58–9. In fairness to the IHA, their initial shocked denial was shared by many; see also Louie Bennett's Statement to the *Report of the Commission on Youth Unemployment 1951* R//82, pp 51–2, and some of the recommendations of the *Commission on Emigration and Other Population Problems 1948–54* (1956), R.84, pp 171–3, and the dissenting retort from Ruaidhri Roberts in his Reservation (No. 11), pp 153–4. This view was not confined to Ireland, either, see Judy Giles, *The Parlour and the Suburb: Domestic Identities, Class, Femininity and Modernity [in post-war Britain]* (Oxford, Berg, 2004).

4 Clear, *House*, pp 1–26.

5 Enda Delaney, *Demography, State and Society: Irish Migration to Britain 1921–1971* (Liverpool, Liverpool University Press, 2000), and Caitríona Clear, 'Too Fond of Going: Female Emigration and Change for Women in Ireland 1946–61', in Dermot Keogh *et al* (eds), *Ireland in the 1950s: The Lost Decade* (Cork, Mercier, 2004), pp 135–46.

6 See e.g. advertisement for probationers for Rush Green hospital, Romford, Essex, *Woman's Life,* 27 January 1951, and advertisment for Bethnal Green and Runwell Mental Hospitals, *Woman's Life,* 24 March 1951, and many more throughout the decade.

7 This was recognized by the *Commission on Emigration.*, and by Muintir na Tire, *The Limerick Rural Survey* (Tipperary, Muintir na Tire Publications, 1964); Eoin O'Leary, 'The INTO and the Marriage Bar for Women National Teachers', *Saothar,* 12 (1987), pp 47–52.

8 For a compendium of these views, see John A. O'Brien (ed), *The Vanishing Irish* (London, W. H. Allen, 1954).

9 Maura Laverty, *Lift Up Your Gates* (London, Longmans, 1946); Laverty's opinion, letter to *The Irish Times,* 12 December 1947. See Caitríona Clear, 'The Red Ink of Emotion: Maura Laverty, Women's Work and Irish Society in the 1940s', *Saothar,* 28 (2003), pp 90–97.

10 Department of Health, National Nutrition Survey Parts I–VII (1948), K.53/1–6.

11 Annual Reports of the Registrar-General, 1923–52: Vital Statistics published annually thereafter. See also Annual Reports of Department of Local Government and Public Health, 1923–47.

12   For Free State/Republic, see discussion in Clear, *House*, pp 96–142; For Northern Ireland, M. Browne and D. S. Johnson, 'Infant Mortality in Inter-War Northern Ireland', in Rosalind Mitchison and Peter Roebuck (eds), *Economy and Society in Scotland and Ireland, 1500–1939* (Edinburgh, John Donald, 1988), pp 277–87.

13   Irvine Loudon, *Death in Childbirth: An International Study of Maternal Care and Infant Mortality 1800–1950* (Oxford, Clarendon Press, 1992); Ruth Barrington, *Health, Medicine and Politics in Ireland 1900–1970* (Dublin, Institute of Public Administration, 1987); Eamonn McKee, 'Church-State Relations and the Development of Irish Health Policy 1944–53', *Irish Historical Studies*, XXV, No. 98 (November 1986).

14   See discussion in Clear, *House*, pp 121–5.

15   See for example the contrasting views of two doctors: Michael Solomons, *Pro-Life? The Irish Question* (Dublin, Lilliput, 1992) p. 6, and John O'Connell, *Doctor John: Crusading Doctor and Politician* (Dublin, Poolbeg, 1989) p. 30.

16   Gerard Kelly S.J. *Medico-Moral Problems* (Dublin, Clonmore and Reynolds, 1955), pp 130–9.

17   Mrs Wyse problem page in *Woman's Life, 1938–59*, and less frequently but still occasionally, Maura Laverty and Angela Macnamara's page in *Woman's Way, 1963–7*.

18   It was a controversial term; see letters' page *Woman's Way*, 30 September 1963, and 2nd fortnight January 1966 for readers who objected to it. Reinforced by personal recollection this author's mother (born 1926, married 1950) and aunts scoffed at the term in the 1960s, associating it, somewhat paradoxically, both with 'posh' women and with being talked down to by advertisers.

19   51.4% of the adult female population were 'engaged in home duties' according to the census of 1936; 54.5% in 1946. Clear, *House*, pp 1–27.

20   The Census, so as not to mask female unemployment by returning too many females as engaged in home duties, only 'allowed' one female thus engaged, unless the household had more than six members (discussion in Clear, *House*, pp 1–27). It is unlikely, therefore, that 'stay-at-home girls' – girls in their teens and twenties happy to be comfortably supported by parents in an idle life, a dwindling minority in any case – accounted for more than a small fraction of these numbers at this time.

WE CAN'T GET ON WITHOUT HOUSEWIVES AND THAT MEANS YOU..

Under 20? We need your youth and enthusiasm.

Under 40? We need your suggestions.

Over 40? We need your time and practical experience.

Join the I.H.A. to-day.

**IRISH HOUSEWIVES ASSOCIATION
5 SOUTH LEINSTER ST., DUBLIN**

Recruitment ad from 1955

HILDA TWEEDY (1911–2005)

Margaret Mac Curtain

Hilda Tweedy was one of a group in twentieth-century Ireland whose firm grasp of the idiom of everyday life enabled them to diagnose the patient's condition with unerring accuracy, and prescribe the cure. A founder-member of the Irish Housewives Association and its historian in her reflective study, *A Link in the Chain* (Attic Press, 1992), in 1942 she and her co-founders were a significant minority who developed for women in Ireland the real meaning of citizenship. The Irish Free State had, by then, become a state where gendered political forces had limited women's access to political and economic power. It was a critical time for the citizens of the Irish Free State. Removed from the theatre of the European war by its constitutional stand on neutrality, the state paid the price in scarcity of money, food and fuel. There was stark poverty in many households and the spectre of tuberculosis struck with deadly effect at families. Children suffered woeful malnutrition with little hope of medical alleviation.

Hilda Tweedy, who had returned from a teaching life in Egypt in 1936, wanted to change that scenario. For her it was not a simple recipe of applying sporadic remedies of 'food-drops', rather it was a searching out of strategies to influence government policy to take requisite action. Of Hilda Tweedy it can be said that she possessed a capacity, not once, but several times in her life for discerning that a time had come when one of her ideas was unstoppable. With a small circle of like-minded women, Andrée Sheehy Skeffington, Marguerite Skelton, Sheila Mallagh and Nancye Simmons in 1941 they formed a pressure group and drew up a petition dubbed 'the housewives petition' and sent copies of it to every member of Dáil Éireann before Budget Day demanding fair prices for producer and consumer and equitable distribution of goods, including food. So government rationing and the book of coupons were introduced, a familiar routine of the Irish citizen's life in the forties. Less than a year later Hilda Tweedy, Andrée Sheehy Skeffington, Susan Manning and Louie Bennett convened the first meeting of the Irish Housewives Association. Over its half-century lifespan, it was one of the most influential voices in consumer affairs, monitoring price-controls, lobbying successive governments, and teaching women to play an active role in community affairs as they impinged on economic policy. The Irish Housewives Association, while not aligning itself with any particular political party, encouraged women to run for office at a period when women's entry into the public sphere had been sharply curtailed.

Sturdily year after year the Association took on the politico-economic establishment confounding their opponents by seeming to glory in their own self-styled appellation 'Irish housewife'. Reproached for their campaign on school meals, Hilda Tweedy recalled one Reverend gentleman who said 'we would be breaking up the sanctity of the home if children were to be fed at school'. Hilda was among those who supported the Minister for Health, Dr Noel Browne in the Mother and Child Scheme. She remembers with amusement a public meeting when her contribution was drowned by an audience who struck up 'Faith of Our Fathers'. Despite rumours that it was pink, the Irish Housewives Association with its energetic executive (Hilda was joint secretary for years and then chairperson, and later still treasurer) developed a solidarity with women's organisations country-wide, forming coalitions that worked as a pressure group if an issue concerning consumer problems arose. Drawing upon remembered tactics which had been used earlier in the suffrage campaigns such as deputations to cabinet ministers, submitting evidence to Dáil committees, writing to county and city councillors, as well as feeding the newspapers with their own press statements, they showed a shrewd sense of where to lean as a lobby. Conscious of the dual role of women in the mid-century they presented to the public the solid frontage of the Irish housewife; strategically they instructed their members on how to negotiate the complex maze of the Irish party machinery.

Some years after stating their aims, the Housewives incorporated the Irish Women Citizens' Association into their membership, thus linking with the older Suffrage Society of 1876, which in 1915 had become the Irish Women's Suffrage and Local Government Association. Hilda Tweedy was justly proud of the continuity between the older radical stream of feminism with the concerns of the new Ireland after the post-war years. How they won recognition from the Trade Union Congress and received affiliation with the International Alliance of Women is part of the story that Hilda Tweedy unfolded in 1992 in *A Link in the Chain*. From early on she had perceived the importance of attending international conferences and between 1946 and 1986 she represented the Irish

Housewives Association so many times at the International Alliance of Women, where she became an important member of the executive, that she truly was one of the best unofficial diplomats Ireland possessed. In writing the history of the association she served so magnificently, Hilda Tweedy brought to light what has remained invisible to leading historians: women's ability to intervene in state policy around price control, and the socialisation of housework in the eyes of the public and the media. Previously in 1931 the Joint Committee of Women's Societies and Social Workers was formed to process issues dealing with social policy and legislation, and the Irish Housewives Association affiliated to that body realising that the sharing of information and experience contributed to the effectiveness of the objective. The Irish Housewives Association supported the Irish Women Laundry Workers' Strike in 1945 which resulted in state recognition of a fortnight's holidays in the year. They taught the 'housewife' to claim her rights, and if she was a member of the Irish Countrywomen's Association, or later in the fifties a member of the Business and Professional Women's Association, then the more powerful the lobby. The coalitions of interest that women developed in the middle decades of the twentieth century prepared the climate for establishing the Council for the Status of Women of which Hilda Tweedy was chairwoman, first of the *ad hoc* committee, 1968–70, and when the Council for the Status of Women was set up she was elected its first chairwoman 1972–78.

Hilda Tweedy would laugh when she was described as a 'redoubtable old-style feminist'. She came from a minority which has played a significant role in defining the nature of Irish feminism. Born in Clones, County Monaghan, she spent her childhood in Athlone where her father was the Church of Ireland rector. Twice in her life she passed through the classrooms of Alexandra College

Dublin, first as pupil and later as teacher – mathematics was her strong interest. Marriage to Robert Tweedy in 1936 brought her back to Dublin and though their three adult children live in different parts of the world, home centred around the house and garden in Stillorgan until their deaths in 2005. Conferred with the degree of Doctor in Laws, *honoris causa*, by Trinity College Dublin in 1990, it was proper that the citation should list among Hilda Anderson Tweedy's achievements her remarkable steadfastness in working to improve the status of women and her work as co-founder and active member of the Irish Housewives Association.

comLacas ban cí na héineann

JOIN THE
Irish Housewives Association
NON-PARTY   NON-SECTARIAN
(Founded 1942)

OBJECT
To unite Housewives so that they may realise, and get recognition for, their right to play an active part in all spheres of planning for the community.

IMMEDIATE AIMS

VIGILANCE ON BEHALF OF CONSUMERS ON

Prices
Food handling
Public health

A FAIR DEAL FOR MOTHERS AND CHILDREN

in matters of Law
Health
Education

WE FIGHT YOUR BATTLES — GIVE US A HAND

Your membership alone is a token of support.
Minimum Annual Subscription 10/-. Life Membership £5.5.0

MEMBERSHIP APPLICATION FORM
I desire to join the Irish Housewives Association and enclose 10/- Minimum Annual Subscription / £5.5.0 Life Membership Subscription (Strike out whichever does not apply).

Name ....

Address ....
To :—
The Hon. Secretaries, The Irish Housewives Association, Basement Flat, 42 Fitzwilliam Place, Dublin 2.

Elo Press Limited : : Dublin 8

Recruitment flyer for the IHA, 1950s

74

HILDA TWEEDY:
A PERSONAL REMINISCENCE

Mary Ryan

"Tis a pity she's a child and not a boy' – these words were uttered by a gardener to the Reverend James Anderson on the birth of Muriel Hilda, the eldest of his three daughters, better known to us as Hilda Tweedy. The gardener's lack of regard for a girl child was deeply mistaken. As it happens, this girl was to become a formidable woman who was a pioneer in many ways, forging her way through the male bastions of power and politics with great success. Hilda Tweedy was not a woman to be tangled with.

Many years ago, I was travelling back by train from my native Galway to my home in Malahide, County Dublin when I read an *Irish Times* article about Hilda. I determined there and then that I would arrange for this amazing woman to speak to my students in Grange Community College, Donaghmede, Dublin 13. This opportunity presented itself when I was co-ordinating a positive ageing programme with transition year students. We hosted a third age (older people) film festival called 'Golden Reels'. There were six films, each of which portrayed third agers in positive and active roles and were screened in UCI Coolock and the Irish Film Institute, Eustace Street, Dublin. A different third age role model was invited to chair an intergenerational discussion after each film. When I phoned Hilda out of the blue (having looked her up in the telephone directory), there was not a second's hesitation before she accepted the invitation to chair a discussion. She came to all six films and on the final day when *Da* was screened in the Irish Film Institute with Hugh Leonard in the chair, Hilda and her husband Robert Tweedy came to lunch with us. A firm relationship began that day between Hilda, Robert, my then partner Kevin Gilmour and myself.

Over the next few years, the relationship was nurtured mostly by long telephone conversations. Hilda was an inveterate telephone person. I think if she were alive now she would be a constant user of the mobile phone. We were soon invited to Sunday lunch. Those afternoons are now wonderful memories of good conversations which ranged from the meaning of poetry (I recall a disagreement between Robert and Gilmour about whether or not free verse could be called poetry – Robert saying that it indeed could not), the political situation in Ireland and globally, stories of Hilda's many trips abroad, details of her politicisation, of the Housewives Petition, the Irish Housewives Association (IHA), the International Alliance of Women (IAW), about how proud she was to have been elected the first Chair of the Council for the Status for Women (CSW), and many personal reminiscences. The lunches were long affairs beginning at about 2.30pm and ending any time around 9 or 10pm. They always began with a dry sherry in Waterford Crystal (Boyne pattern) sherry glasses – Hilda's favourite was Tio Pepe and it became mine too – and nibbles to be followed by Hilda's wonderful lunch. Naturally nothing came out of a packet.

My favourites were the upside-down pudding and pears marinated in red wine.

Hilda told us of the many encounters she had had with politicians – grey-suited men like Charlie Haughey who thought that women would go away if token gestures were extended in their direction. She sometimes gave a different perspective on what politicians had claimed as their own initiatives, e.g. the free transport for older people. Hilda told us that the IHA were the first to moot this notion, yet a male politician is credited with it. Those with whom she negotiated had not realised that Hilda's petite stature belied a steely determination and a dogged tenacity. She often spoke of the poverty she saw on the streets of Dublin in the 1930s, 1940s and 1950s and how it spurred her on to give a whole new meaning to the role of housewife. Suffice to say I often regretted not having a tape recorder secreted in the dining-room somewhere to record the fascinating minutiae. I had talked about taping her and she had hesitated too many times for me to persist. Sadly, on my penultimate visit to Hilda in St Vincent's Hospital, she told me to bring my dictaphone on the next trip. I did arrive with it to discover Hilda was dying. We exchanged few words during that visit and I am privileged that she reached out for my hand and we remained hand-in-hand until her children Robert and Jean arrived and I gently extricated my hand from hers to make room for them at the bedside. It was my last encounter with a great friend.

The last years of my friendship with Hilda and Robert were a threesome, as Gilmour and I had separated. I mention it here because it is important to record what wonderful support both of them gave me in my hour of need. Not long after my separation, I opened the door one day to find the local florist with a bunch of red roses bearing a message of support and love; Hilda told me that it was Robert's idea. In 1996–97 I did an MA in Equality Studies in UCD. On the first morning of the course, I received a copy of Hilda's *A Link in the Chain: The Story of the Irish Housewives Association, 1942–1992* with a message of encouragement inside. That was Hilda Tweedy: thoughtful, supportive and positively reinforcing.

I often spent Saturday night with Hilda and Robert. Once on my way back from Galway, I got delayed because I'd put diesel in the car rather than petrol ... I arrived about 10pm, slightly nervous of Robert's reaction to my stupidity, only to be greeted with a warm hug from each of them. I felt cosseted. Those Saturday nights and the following mornings were a source of great pleasure for me. Hilda and Robert always took a nap after tea time and got up about 7.30pm full of energy and chat. We would talk and have supper and talk some more; bedtime was relatively late. I was always told the night before to stay in bed and rest in the morning and I did, emerging some time around 10am to find Hilda and Robert waiting for me to have breakfast. There was no fuss about it. I was given Jean's room and how I loved that soft, warm bed with the blankets. I was transported back to my childhood before duvets and I felt all the security and love underneath the blankets that I had felt in my parents' house.

During the summer of 2000, I spent the night before my first trip to a Marxist conference in London with Hilda and Robert. I was leaving early in the morning and knew that I could tell Hilda where I was going, but was in dread of telling Robert because of his possible reaction to radical politics. I will never forget the smile that quickly spread across Robert's face when I told him. He was delighted to hear I am a socialist. He told me about how his father, affectionately known as Pop Tweedy, had once been a communist. The three of us had a wonderful, long discussion about the evils of capitalism, the fears around communism and the possibilities of creating some kind of equality under socialism. Incidentally, Robert's father reverted to socialism once he saw what was going on in Soviet Russia.

By the year 2000, I was working in Castleknock Community College (CCC) and the challenges of immigration were being experienced in Irish society. We in CCC decided that we needed to manifest our intolerance of racism and our positive attitude towards immigrants. We held a competition for the design of what we then called a Refugee Solidarity Badge. Twin brothers won the competition and were helped to professionalise the badge by the well-known artist Robert Ballagh. Hilda was absolutely thrilled with the idea and immediately became involved in the project. The badge was launched in the Hugh Lane Gallery by Mary Robinson, then United Nations High Commissioner for Human Rights. Hilda took it on with a passion and a commitment and sold it at every event she attended over the next few years. She invited a number of her friends including myself to her house with the intention of establishing a committed group of people who would disseminate the badge widely. Unfortunately, the ill-health of Robert and later of Hilda herself stood in the way. But by then, Hilda had already sold hundreds of badges.

I met many interesting people in Hillcrest (the Tweedy house in Stillorgan, County Dublin) many of them members of the International Alliance of Women (IAW). The IAW is a non-governmental, feminist organisation, which embraces both women's groups and individuals. Its basic principle is that the full and equal enjoyment of human rights is due to all women and girls and its objective is to become the global voice of women who want to make a difference. The decision for the establishment of the organisation was taken in Washington in 1902. The Alliance was formally constituted in Berlin in 1904 as the International Woman Suffrage Alliance, and adopted its current name 'International Alliance of Women: Equal Rights – Equal Responsibilities' in 1946. The IAW represents more than 50 organisations worldwide and has attracted many individual members; all of those whom I met with Hilda were intelligent focused women and some believed in radical politics. The Irish Housewives Association became affiliated to the International Alliance of Women in 1948 and became involved in issues such as reproductive rights.

I felt very privileged when one evening Hilda told me that her two confidantes were Sr Margaret Mac Curtain and myself. In an organic way, we exchanged stories. Mine have gone to the grave with Hilda; Hilda's will go to the grave with me. Suffice to say that Hilda dealt with life's vicissitudes in a constructive and pragmatic way. There were many stories which were not secret. Hilda often talked about her life in Alexandria, Egypt and how she set up a school in which she taught. We spent an evening going through a trunk in which were stored her beautiful wedding veil and a few evening dresses. There was a story with each dress. I was often transported to Hilda's life before her marriage.

Hilda was very proud and possessive of her kitchen. She was very particular about whom she allowed into it. I was gratified when one day she told me that of the people who had helped her in her kitchen, I was the one who seemed to know where each utensil and tool was stored. I guess this is because, like Hilda, I hate things being out of place.

There were so many things I loved about Hilda: her determination, her empathy, her tenacity, her gentleness and above all the fact that I never had to edit my thoughts when talking to her. She crossed time lines and was never judgemental. She liked me for who I am; it did not matter if my phone calls to her were not as frequent as they should have been because of my busy life. We always took up from where we left off. It was a pleasure and privilege to have shared so many hours with Hilda Anderson Tweedy. Often when I am making a decision which may not have popular appeal, I wonder what Hilda would have done.

Of all her qualities, the one which impressed me most was her courage. Hilda and Robert lived in a secluded bungalow in Stillorgan. The last few years of their lives were cruelly punctuated by break-ins and robberies. Hilda and Robert never reacted in a frightened or nervous way. I recall one incident in particular when a man called to the door with a false identity card saying he was from the county council and was in the area to check the water supply. Hilda let him in and, of course, behind him two or three other men forced their way into the house. On hearing them, Robert stood up (by this time Robert was blind and quite deaf) calling out to Hilda 'who is there?' but was pushed roughly back into his armchair. The men began questioning them about where there might be money. Suddenly Hilda saw her opportunity – she whacked her interrogator as hard as she could across the shins with her walking stick. While he was bent over in pain, she darted out of the dining room and ran to the bedroom where was a panic button. She reached it before the man could catch up on her. Luckily for Hilda and Robert, the men made a quick getaway without touching them. Instead of congratulating herself for her brave deed, Hilda berated herself for having allowed the man in. She was not for intimidating!

Having had Hilda in my life has been a most positive experience. She is one of my role models and there is even the added bonus of having 'adopted' two of Hilda's close friends as my own. Her beliefs and commitments brought her across geographic, social, age and class boundaries. In essence, she believed in and worked towards human rights for all women and girls. Sometimes I give thanks that she has not lived to see the debacle surrounding the Irish banks. Some of her ancestors were bankers and she was proud of that, but even before she died, she regretted the change in the banking ethos from commitment to the individual to indulging big business. How would she have reacted to our current situation as she watched many of the reforms which she and her companions helped to bring about being gradually eroded as a result of the banking misdemeanours?

Society needs people like Hilda Tweedy. Let us hope that history books give her space commensurate with her achievements so that younger people can aspire to have the kind of society which Hilda wanted, one where women's work is counted and respected, rather than taken for granted and where there is true equality between women and men.

REMEMBERING HILDA AND ANDRÉE AND THEIR WORK

Rosemary Cullen Owens

In 1974, I commenced research for an MA thesis on the history of the Irish women's suffrage movement from the 1870s to the establishment of the Irish Free State in 1922. Finding only limited material available in our libraries at this stage, I set about contacting any relatives of the women who had been suffrage activists. My first call was to Andrée Sheehy Skeffington, French-born daughter-in-law of the prominent feminist Hanna Sheehy Skeffington. Andrée was most hospitable, and a fount of knowledge. In addition, her house was full to the brim of archives belonging to Hanna and her husband Frank, and Andrée's late husband Owen Sheehy Skeffington.

The United Nations designated 1975 as International Women's Year, and immediately Andrée set about organising an exhibition on the Irish Women's Suffrage Movement to be shown in Trinity College, Dublin. Very quickly, I found myself drawn in to help with the organisation of the exhibition. While time consuming, this experience was very beneficial for my research. In addition to her family papers and memorabilia – much of which she put on show at the exhibition – Andrée was very generous with her time in answering my many questions regarding the individuals involved in the women's campaign. When the exhibition ended, I had a number of chats with Andrée about her life in Ireland since 1935. During one of these chats, she mentioned that she and a group of friends had formed the Irish Housewives Association in 1942, in reaction to the plight of the poor due to the shortage of everyday food items and the lack of rationing. The other key founder of the Irish Housewives Association she told me was Hilda Tweedy.

At this point, I have a confession to make. While I knew the Sheehy Skeffington name from my suffrage research, I knew little of Hilda Tweedy. Yes, I had heard of the Irish Housewives Association, but as a young woman in the mid-1970s, with 'Women's Lib', equal pay and equality issues dominating the media, the Irish Housewives' name conjured up an image of a conservative, non-radical organisation. How wrong could I have been!

During my first few meetings with Hilda during the 1980s, we discussed any women she had known who had been active in the suffrage campaign. In particular we discussed Louie Bennett who post-1916 had devoted her life to the organisation of women workers, including laundry workers. Hilda's husband Robert was very helpful also in this regard, having managed the Court Laundry in Harcourt Street for many years, during which time he had much contact with Ms Bennett.

Prior to the formation of the Irish Housewives Association, Dr Bob Collis, a Dublin paediatrician, pointed out that Dublin contained the foulest slums in Europe, and that the plight of the poor in the city was appalling, with ninety thousand living in one-roomed tenements without a proper water supply. His play, *Marrowbone Lane*, provided an important stimulus to these young women and their emerging political consciousness. In 1944 the new Chief Medical Adviser to the Department of Local Government and Public Health, Dr James Deeny, highlighted some of the challenges facing him:

> We had the worst tuberculosis problem in Western Europe, the last louse-bourne typhus in Western Europe, a chronic typhoid problem, a very high infant mortality rate with huge numbers of babies dying from enteritis, a high maternal mortality rate … And of course there was a war on.[1]

The number of children dying from enteritis rose to 1,000 per year from 1941, six hundred of these in Dublin alone. Deeney's work revealed that the disease was related to poverty, overcrowding and the domestic infection of foods, particularly milk. Rickets was another serious health concern, caused by a shortage of calcium in the diet of the poor. In an address to the Women's Social and Political League (WSPL) in the spring of 1940, Collis emphasised the need to reduce food prices to the poor. Citing research on the wives of unemployed men attending the Rotunda ante-natal clinic, based on minimum standards laid down by the League of Nations, he pointed out that only 6% of such women were receiving enough protective food and only 8% received enough food of any kind; 'on average they were only getting half the minimum amount of food they required, and were, literally, in a state of semi-starvation'.

The outbreak of World War II exacerbated all these conditions. While the Irish Free State was removed from direct involvement in the war through its neutrality stance, it nonetheless suffered severe shortage of imported goods such as tea, flour and fuel. During the years of the 'Emergency', prices soared and goods became prohibitively expensive. The cost of living rose by two-thirds, while wages rose by one-third. Emmet O'Connor has written that 'Unemployment, poverty, and above all, the social inequality of the Emergency regime, swung public opinion to the left'.[2] Dr. James Deeny wrote:

> Wet turf with which to cook and heat, a short daily period of gas 'glimmer', shortages, deprivation and poverty. Wartime for the Lurgan people was relative prosperity; for the Dublin poor, it meant that their poverty and misery grew worse.[3]

Aware of the problems outlined above Hilda decided she would like to do something about the situation. She asked a small group of friends to her home to see what ideas they might come up with. A couple of days before this meeting she began to get cold feet, afraid that they would just become another well-meaning group. She recalled thinking of their friends, the Skeffingtons. Aware of Andrée's experience in research and organisation, Hilda called her to ask if she would come to the meeting to try to put a shape on it. When the women met, they drew up a petition on fair prices for producer and consumer, and fair distribution of goods. The petition was sent to the government for Budget Day, 5 May 1941. Initially signed by 51 women – a figure which grew to 640 – the petition was also presented to the opposition parties and the press the day before the budget. High on the list of the petition was a request for national registration of all essential foodstuffs, with immediate and effective rationing to sell goods at standard prices within reach of all. The issue of equality of such rationing was paramount in their demands. They also called for a government fruit and vegetable market to supply retailers and control retail prices, control on the production and distribution of food with fair prices for producer and consumer, and similar controls on the production, distribution and consumption of fuels, gas and electricity.

The petition caught the imagination of the press, which gave it much coverage, dubbing it the 'Housewives

Petition'. Hilda felt that the press tried to put them down with this title – after all what would mere housewives know of such things? Andrée felt that the action of the newspapers presented a challenge to women as homemakers 'to speak up for women in the home'. Louie Bennett and her sister Susan Manning (signatories to the petition) advised the group's leaders to build on the momentum generated by the petition to start a new women's organisation, Bennett offering the use of the Irish Women Workers' Union (IWWU) hall for an inaugural meeting. In May 1942, with an initial membership of 12, the Irish Housewives Committee was formed, the title being amended in 1946 to the Irish Housewives Association. Susan Manning became the first Chairman (the title used at that time), with Hilda and Andrée elected as joint honorary secretaries. While Andrée's mother-in-law had reservations about the title of the new organisation commenting 'you are not married to the house you know', Andrée's mantra for the IHA became 'educate, investigate, agitate', a *modus operandi* at which the group became particularly adept.

Citing Andrée as the one who really knew what they should be doing, Hilda explained that the IHA now started to lobby politicians on various issues of interest to women and children. In something of a throwback to the poster parades of the suffrage era, the IHA marched through Dublin with posters stating 'The Children Must be Fed', 'War on TB', 'Pure Milk', 'Clean Food', Fair Prices', and 'Give the Children Dinner and not Bread'.[4] School managers, doctors, TDs and members of Dublin Corporation were all lobbied in its campaign for a hot meal and one third of a pint of milk daily for school children.

Hilda noted that very quickly the IHA saw that women needed power to make their voices heard. They endorsed

Hanna's candidature as an independent candidate for the Dáil in 1943. By 1946, despite her reservations with the title of 'housewife', Hanna now applauded the achievements of 'a band of energetic and determined women in ending the black market and obtaining price controls'. She urged further education and organisation in citizenship, commenting with humour:

The Association needs more members, additional subscribers, investigators, workers, politically minded women – much work remains to be done in '46. Go to it, housewives![5]

There had been a huge rise in the cost of living during the war years. In 1946 the wages freeze was abolished and the Labour Court established. Pay increases would now be negotiated through this Court. Trade unionists were concerned that further pay increases would be offset by price increases. Christy Ferguson of the Workers' Union of Ireland (WUI) proposed that the Dublin Trade Union Council invite labour bodies and women's organisations to a conference, for the purpose of initiating a campaign for the immediate control of prices. This conference was held in January 1947 and attended by the IHA, WSPL, Labour Party and Clann na Poblachta. From this conference emerged the Lower Prices Council (LPC) with E.J Tucker of the TUC as Chairman and Maureen O'Carroll as Hon. Secretary. In addition to trade union and labour representation, the IHA, the WSPL, and the Joint Committee of Women's Societies and Social Workers (JCWSSW) were also represented. In recognition of the work done by the IHA in the area of price control Hilda Tweedy was elected as Honorary Secretary of the executive co-ordinating committee. A contemporary newspaper reported that 'every morning Mrs Maureen O'Carroll goes shopping for 70,000 people, knowing what the price of everything from food to fuel should be'. The report noted that when an instance of overcharging is discovered, the LPC buys the article concerned, sending the receipt to the Department of Industry and Commerce for action; Mrs O'Carroll (later to be a Labour TD and mother of the comedian Brendan O'Carroll) commenting that they gave no second chances, even if the overcharge was only a farthing. When questioned about the methods used to maintain its 'incessant research into costs of production', Mrs. O'Carroll responded mysteriously, 'we have our own methods'.[6]

In October 1947 the LPC organised what became known as 'the Women's Parliament' in Dublin's Mansion House. Participating women were allocated ministerial portfolios as re-enforcement of their right to commentate on the national housekeeping. Louie Bennett chaired this meeting. Myles na gCopaleen wrote in *The Irish Times*:

It says in the papers that more than 300,000 women in every county in Ireland will be represented at the Women's Parliament in Dublin – *to demand* – if you don't mind, 'control of prices and an immediate reduction in the cost of essential goods and other commodities'. Hah? I well remember the day, and your poor father would bear me out in this, when into the newspapers the word 'women' never got! In those days respectability was the rage of course.[7]

The aim of achieving more politically minded women members was strengthened in 1947 when the Irish Women Citizens Association (formerly the Irish Women's Suffrage and Local Government Association) was incorporated into the IHA. The IWCA could trace its roots back to the first Dublin suffrage society formed in 1876 by Anna and Thomas Haslam. During the intervening years the association had obtained Poor Law Guardianship, and Local Government and the Parliamentary franchise for women.

An important result of this incorporation was the formation of an international committee of the IHA with members from both organisations dedicated to carry on the work of the IWCA through its affiliation to the International Alliance of Women (IAW). Lucy Kingston played a key role in this transition, having been involved in the earlier suffrage campaign and later in the IWCA. The IAW had been formed in 1902 by suffragists from the US, Europe and Australia. It held regular conferences in Europe and the US at which wide-ranging discussion on women's issues took place. From 1947, this international connection would prove vital in expanding the knowledge and expectations of both the IHA and Irish women's groups generally on issues of equality and rights. In 1946 the IAW changed its name to 'International Alliance of Women: Equal Rights – Equal Responsibilities'. The IAW is still in existence, with consultative status to the UN Economic and Social Council and participatory status with the Council of Europe.

Hilda was particularly supportive of this development on the part of the IHA, and in the course of attending many of its conferences, she and other IHA members became aware of the broad spectrum of women's issues being addressed by the IAW in different countries. It was through its affiliation to the IAW that the IHA established a link with the UN Commission on the Status of Women. IHA delegates to the IAW's 1967 congress in London learned that this UN Commission had issued a directive to women's international non-governmental organisations asking affiliates to examine the status of women in their own countries and, where necessary, urge their governments to set up a national commission on the status of women. At the same time, the Business and Professional Women's Clubs (BPWC), attending another European congress, heard of the new development. This news set in train a chain of events that would dramatically change the status of women in Ireland.

The IHA and the BPWC decided to work together on the setting up of such a commission. After a meeting in Dublin in January 1968 attended by representatives of a dozen women's groups, it was decided to establish an Ad Hoc Committee to work for a limited period, researching the need for a national commission. Hilda was elected Chair of this committee, with nine other women's groups and one independent woman, Rosaleen Mills, represented on the committee. Following intensive research by the committee on a wide range of issues relating to women, a memorandum was sent to the Taoiseach, Jack Lynch, by the Ad Hoc Committee in October 1968. They were left waiting more than a year for a response. On 7 November 1969, a reply was received from Mr Lynch stating that he was recommending the setting up of a National Commission on the Status of Women. At the suggestion of the Ad Hoc Committee, Dr Thekla Beere was appointed Chair of the National Commission. In 1971 the Commission published an interim report on Equal Pay, its full report being published in 1972. To ensure implementation of the Commission's recommendations, and to act as a co-ordinating body for women's organisations, a permanent Council for the Status of Women was established in 1972. Hilda was its first chairperson, a role she held for six years.

Hilda was particularly proud of the role the IHA formed as a continuous bond in the women's movement from the 1870s to the 1970s. When I asked if she considered herself a feminist, her answer was a resounding yes. She commented that different strands of feminism were now coming together than before, some more radical than others. She reminded me that in its early days the IHA was considered very radical. When she looked back at the significant achievements of the early feminists between 1870–1920, I think she was happy that through their work from the 1940s the IHA and the IWCA had done justice to those pioneers, and earned a place as their successors.

Another important concern between both groups was a commitment to pacifism. World War I had caused division between suffrage groups internationally. In 1915 the Women's International League for Peace and Freedom (WILPF) was formed in The Hague by suffragists from Europe and North America in protest against the war. An Irish branch of the League was formed by leading suffrage activists, remaining in existence until 1931. Louie Bennett and Lucy Kingston, both confirmed pacifists, were very active in WILPF, and in the organisation of its fifth interational congress which was held in Dublin in 1926. In 1991, WILPF in Ireland was reconstituted in protest at the Gulf War. As one of the initiators of this event, I was very happy when Hilda appeared at one of our meetings, and continued to give us her support and advice. This she saw as another example of continuing in the footsteps of early women activists.

On a personal note, having first met Hilda and Andrée during the course of my MA research, I ended up with more than just a degree. I became friends with two of the most remarkable women I have known. I was lucky in such friendship, and remember my frequent visits to both their homes. In Andrée's, there was always a welcoming pot of tea, and often lunch. I remember her mother coming to live with her. I don't remember her speaking much English, and I don't know what she made of my very amateur French. In Hilda's home there was similar hospitality, and great discussions with both Hilda and Robert. They had a beautiful garden, and Robert knew every plant by its correct botanical name.

With Dublin being the small city it is, I discovered connections between myself and the two households. Andrée's late husband Owen had attended the same school my sons were then attending, and if memory serves me correctly, I think Robert Tweedy had spent some time at that school when it was under different management. In addition, after Robert retired from the Court Laundry, in 1962 he and Hilda established an educational toyshop, 'Nimble Fingers', which they ran until 1982. I discovered an in-law of my husband's had then bought the business, and it is still run by that family. Above all, though, I remember the frequent phone calls from Hilda. When I was going through a particularly difficult time in my life, she would call me regularly to find out how I was doing, and to let me know she was there for me.

NOTES

1   James Deeny, *To Cure and to Care: Memoirs of a Chief Medical Officer* (Dublin, Glendale, 1989), pp 73–4.

2   Emmet O'Connor, *A Labour History of Ireland 1824–1960* (Dublin, Gill and Macmillan, 1992), p. 137.

3   Deeny, p. 98.

4   Finola Kennedy, *Cottage to Creche: Family Change in Ireland* (Dublin, Institute of Public Administration, 2001) p. 107.

5   Quoted in Margaret Ward, *Hanna Sheehy Skeffington: A Life* (Cork, Attic Press, 1997), pp 343–4.

6   Cited in Seamus Cody, John O'Dowd, Peter Rigney (eds), *The Parliament of Labour: 100 Years of the Dublin Council of Trade Unions* (Dublin, Women's Community Press, 1986), p. 192.

7   Myles na gCopaleen, cited in Cody, O'Dowd, Rigney (eds), p. 193.

Monica Sheridan (right) addressing an audience of housewives and
some interested men at the Pigs and Bacon Commission, 1960s

The IHA and the Introduction of Rationing in Ireland

Bryce Evans

'For the Community, Not for Profit': this simple slogan, coined by Hilda Tweedy, sums up the role of the Irish Housewives Association during the Emergency. Launched at a time when *moral* considerations infused many facets of everyday life in Ireland, the IHA's assault on the *material* deprivation of the period remains impressive. Much has been written about the moral dimension of Irish neutrality between 1939 and 1945.[1] And yet, for the majority of Irish people, this policy mattered little in abstract but plenty in terms of its material effects.[2]

Put in base material terms, the implications of staying out of the Anglo-American war effort were clear. Neutrality meant that Ireland did not receive Allied help in the form of food and fuel shipments. This resulted in crippling supply shortages for the duration of the conflict. The Fianna Fáil government's 'Wages Standstill Order' of May 1941 aggravated these hardships: the cost of living rose considerably due to wartime inflation, but wages remained low.[3]

Today, the statue of James Larkin on Dublin's O'Connell Street, his huge hands outthrust, provides a powerful physical reminder of the tensions caused by these conditions. Larkin's opposition to the Trade Union Bill of June 1941, which the statue captures, is the most famous symbol of collective working class discontent during the Emergency and signified the worst crisis in government-trade union relations since independence. But of Hilda Tweedy and the Irish Housewives Association – arguably as effective as Larkin in ensuring that the Irish state looked after the basic material needs of its people in this period – there is no statue to admire.

Tweedy claimed that 'women are apt to grumble about high prices and food scarcities but too slow to realise their duty to try to remedy these social evils'.[4] Statements such as this, which place the emphasis on a voluntary, 'step together' spirit, can mask the radicalism of the movement somewhat. But if Tweedy was frustrated with the greed and petty racketeering that she observed in her social circle, her passionate cause was the alleviation of urban poverty and malnutrition during the Emergency. These 'social evils', as she recognised, may have been compounded by the selfishness of some, but were fundamentally caused by government inaction in a time of crisis.

The IHA's well publicised 1941 memorandum exhibited some markedly socialist tendencies, calling on the government to institute a fair price for producers and consumers, a minimum wage for workers, greater market regulation, communal feeding centres and 'the suppression of all black markets'.[5] The memorandum, or the 'Housewives' Petition' as the press dubbed it, was a landmark document in both its vision of a comprehensive and state-directed moral economy, its exposure of urban squalor, and – crucially – its impact on government.

Before the submission of the petition, Ireland's rationing system was patchy. It was overseen by Seán Lemass, the youngest (and widely regarded as the ablest) member of Éamon de Valera's cabinet. Previously Minister for Industry and Commerce, Lemass was appointed the new Minister of Supplies in September 1939. His new department was equipped with an extraordinarily interventionist *raison d'etre*: to secure effective and equitable distribution for as long as Emergency conditions prevailed. The state's meticulous censorship network kept Supplies informed of instances of profiteering, speculation and evasion of orders,[6] and as the department grew in size and personnel Lemass assumed an unprecedented degree of control over economic life. He had the power to fix the prices and quantities of all commodities, dictating the methods of 'treatment, keeping, storage, movement, distribution, sale, purchase, use and consumption' of all goods.[7] Lemass's wide-ranging economic powers at this time have earned him the title 'economic overlord' and 'dictator' by admiring historians.[8]

For all his powers, though, Lemass had only instituted a system of *partial* rationing by the time the IHA was being organised. The state would not be the only economic actor during the Emergency, Lemass insisted, in defending this system. In their consumer activity and in their market practices the people of Ireland were responsible, he claimed, for the economic wellbeing of the country. In radio announcements on the supply position Lemass urged women to exercise self-restraint in their consumption of key goods such as butter, tea, coal and petrol and stated that he did not want to introduce a full rationing system.[9] Frequently asserting the need for the public to practice frugality, Lemass stated that the government had neither the resources nor the organisation to overcome the supply crisis without the co-operation of the public.[10] 'Voluntary measures of economy' were preferable to full rationing, he asserted, asking for the 'voluntary assistance of every housewife' in reducing consumption.[11]

In submitting the famous petition, Tweedy and her fellow activists bravely exposed the uncomfortable truth that such a well-meaning system was simply not working and that Lemass was using his considerable powers ineffectively. The public were resorting to the black market out of necessity, avarice, but also – and most significantly – confusion. Lemass expected the public to adhere to price control orders published daily in the censored wartime press; but in an economic environment shaped by the uncertain progress of war, such orders were issued so frequently that they became almost meaningless. Lemass's announcements on the price of coal exemplify the difficulties he faced in attempting to instill a moral economic ethic in the public without the accompaniment of a comprehensive rationing system and coherent price structure. On 20 September 1939, shortly after the outbreak of war, he announced that coal could not be sold at any price over an extra *two* shillings per ton on the price outlined in a Price Standstill Order he had issued a week beforehand.[12] The following day, 21 September, he announced that coal could now not be sold at any price over an extra *five* shillings per ton on the original price.[13]

As inflation spiraled, such constant addition and removal of price orders and regulatory measures on goods led to accusations of complacency on Lemass's behalf. He was 'chopping and changing' on food prices to the people's detriment, it was claimed in the Dáil.[14] It was stated elsewhere that he was incompetent in the face of the 'soaring prices of the very essentials of existence'.[15] The example of coal prices came in the early stages of war; the situation was to get much worse as Britain exerted a harsh supply squeeze from late 1940 onwards. People remained baffled as to the legal price of goods and were desperately in need of basic foodstuffs. Meanwhile, the black market boomed. 'The poor are like hunted rats looking for bread' remarked Fine Gael TD Richard Mulcahy of the miserably long queues which developed across Ireland as food supplies dwindled.[16]

The IHA's memorandum was published in May 1941, coinciding with Lemass's private decision to replace the rather haphazard early system with formal rationing in Ireland. The timing implies that as a document of radical consumer dissatisfaction it acted as the sort of firm stimulus needed to change Lemass's mind on rationing at a time when he was dithering over the introduction of coherent social and economic measures to deal with the crisis of supplies and black marketing. Despite the plight of the urban poor, Lemass did not publicly announce the introduction of comprehensive rationing of essential foodstuffs until January 1942 and ration books were not delivered until May of that year. Notwithstanding the immense effort involved in the processing and collection of data for rationing, this was a delayed reaction to a situation which had been getting progressively worse since the fall of France in June 1940. The women who went on to establish the IHA in 1942, to their credit, had called for such a move since early 1941.

Hilda Tweedy and the IHA were therefore influential in transforming the material experience of the Emergency for the Irish people. From the outset, they challenged the system instituted by the government whereby people registered at their local shop to exchange coupons for certain items, questioning whether 'a voluntary curtailment of consumption' was working and calling instead for the comprehensive system of rationing that would later be instituted.[17] The IHA pointed to Britain's formal rationing as a model and contended that the poorest and largest families could not survive on the government's meagre food and clothing allowances. Neither was the submission of the petition its only success in terms of policy. The organisation continued to lobby for the introduction of a range of measures and, in the case of free milk for children and price controls on cooking fats in 1944, these calls were heeded by government.[18]

Intent on rescuing a moral economy from the teeth of the black economy in Ireland's urban centres, the IHA were a thorn in Lemass's side for the long course of the Emergency. IHA members marched through Dublin in March 1942 with placards that read 'The Children Must be Fed' and 'Fair Prices'.[19] In 1945 the organisation complained that the government was not only too lenient on profiteers but had taken too long to enforce the necessary restrictions on a domestic market squeezed by shortages.[20] As the Emergency continued and the market tightened, the influence of other pressure groups urging government control over the black market increased, all inspired by the boldness of the IHA and Hilda Tweedy.

On the other hand, it is important to note that the IHA's anti-black market views were not entirely representative of Irish society during the Emergency. While the Irish Housewives tapped into the popular mood of resentment towards excessive profiteering, their abstinence from more modest involvement with the black market was exceptional. A senior figure in the Fianna Fáil hierarchy, Todd Andrews, relates how his wife Mary (a member of the IHA) broke off social relations with friends who had treated her to bread and cakes made from black market white flour.[21] While laudable, it is important to note that Mrs Andrews had the luxury to take this decision whereas poor and working class mothers in Ireland's towns and cities were often forced to rely on the black market to feed their families. Despite campaigning on their behalf, the IHA was typically not composed of the mothers of the poorest and largest families and by Tweedy's own admission it was a 'predominately Protestant, middle class venture'.[22] While the IHA possessed many middle class members of similar conviction to Tweedy, many other members of the middle class used their relatively strong purchasing power to stock up in advance of scarcity.

Nonetheless, the contribution of the Irish Housewives Association to popular protest as well as the management of Ireland's Emergency was decisive. The civil servants in Lemass's department, however, were not going to admit as much. After the war, the department's officials composed a lengthy history of the short-lived Department of Supplies, intended as a guide which civil servants and ministers occupying a similar brief in any future conflict would be able to consult. In these surviving records of the Department of Supplies and, consequently, in economic and political histories of the Emergency, the IHA was all but written out of history. Yet despite the conspicuous omission of its influence, the IHA was the most active and radical voluntary organisation to combat the effects of shortages in urban Ireland during the Emergency: a time when Tweedy's cry 'For the Community, Not for Profit' sounded clearly and powerfully alongside Larkin's booming oratory.

NOTES

1   See Robert Fisk, *In Time of War: Ireland, Ulster and the Price of Neutrality 1939–45* (London, Andre Deutsch, 1983); Donal Ó Drisceoil, *Censorship in Ireland, 1939–1945: Neutrality, Politics, and Society* (Cork, Cork University Press, 1996); Dermot Keogh and Mervyn O'Driscoll (eds), *Ireland in World War Two:*

Neutrality and Survival (Cork, Mercier Press, 2004). For a critical take on the policy of neutrality see Brian Girvin, *The Emergency: Neutral Ireland 1939–45* (London, Macmillan, 2006).

2   For other works discussing the material impact of war on ordinary Irish people see Gerard Fee, 'The Effects of World War II on Dublin's Low-Income Families, 1939–1945' (unpublished PhD thesis, UCD, 1996); Lindsey Earner-Byrne, *Mother and Child: Maternity and Child Welfare in Ireland, 1920s–1960s* (Manchester, Manchester University Press, 2007); Mary Muldowney *The Second World War and Irish Women: An Oral History* (Dublin, Irish Academic Press, 2007); Clair Wills, *That Neutral Island: A Cultural History of Ireland During the Second World War* (London, Faber, 2007).

3   For statistical accounts of the extent to which prices outstripped wages see Liam Kennedy, *Modern Industrialisation of Ireland 1940–1988* (Dublin, The Economic and Social History Society of Ireland, 1989), p. 6; Mary E. Daly, *Social and Economic History of Ireland since 1800* (Dublin, Educational Company, 1981), p. 157.

4   Hilda Tweedy to Women's Social and Progressive League, 11 November 1943. National Archives of Ireland (NAI), Tweedy Papers, JUS/98/17/5/1/2.

5   Irish Housewives Association, 'Memorandum on the Food and Fuel Emergency', 5 May 1941. NAI, Tweedy Papers, JUS/98/17/5/1/1.

6   Ó Drisceoil, *Censorship*, p. 61.

7   Department of Supplies, 'Record of Activities'. NAI, IND/EHR/3/15, appendix I.

8   The terms were employed, respectively, by Ronan Fanning and Liam Skinner. For an overview of the historiography of Lemass as Minister of Supplies see Bryce Evans, *Seán Lemass: Democratic Dictator* (Cork, The Collins Press, 2011), p. 113.

9   *Munster Express*, 15 November 1940.

10   *Meath Chronicle*, 13 July 1940.

11   *Irish Independent*, 12 October 1940.

12   *Irish Press*, 20 September, 1939.

13   *Irish Press*, 21 September, 1939.

14   *Irish Independent*, 9 November, 1939.

15   *Southern Star*, 18 November, 1939.

16   Wills, *That Neutral Island*, p. 241.

17   *Irish Times*, 22 February, 1942.

18   NAI, Tweedy Papers, 98/17/5/1/2.
19   'Irish Housewives Protest', 13 March 1942. NAI, Tweedy Papers, JUS/98/17/5/1/3.
20   'Evidence of the Irish Housewives Before the Milk Tribunal', NAI, Tweedy Papers, JUS/98/17/5/1/6.
21   C.S. Andrews, *Man of No Property* (Dublin, Lilliput Press, 2001), p. 329.
22   Hilda Tweedy, *A Link in the Chain* (Dublin, Attic Press, 1992), p. 15.

The Irish Housewife, 1957

UNDERCOVER OF *THE IRISH HOUSEWIFE*: A WOMEN'S MAGAZINE FOR A NEW AGE

Sonja Tiernan

Many organisations in Ireland's past have produced newsletters, magazines and journals to express the ethos of their society. On the surface, journals such as the *Irish Homestead* or the *Catholic Bulletin* appear innocent or possibly even mundane to club outsiders. An article on treating cattle scour was hardly an appeal to buy a copy of the *Irish Homestead*, unless this was a pertinent issue to the reader. However, the content of these publications was not always as it first appeared. The radical nature of these publications is perhaps most evident in the pages of Ireland's first women's periodical, *Bean na hÉireann*. The official magazine of Maud Gonne's organisation Inghinidhe na hÉireann, it was described by its editor, Helena Molony, as 'a funny hotch-potch of blood and thunder, high thinking, and home-made bread'.[1] Similarly, the first official publication of the Irish Housewives Association, *The Irish Housewife*, contains an eclectic mix of articles. The title portrays a publication which might include cookery pages, knitting patterns and tips on running an efficient household. The magazine includes all of this, but so much more.

This article provides an overview of *The Irish Housewife*, published from 1946 until after the Silver Jubilee of the Irish Housewives Association in 1967. The magazine was the initiative of IHA co-founder, Andrée Sheehy Skeffington.[2] Hilda Tweedy took a prominent position on the editorial board from the first issue.[3] The board procured articles by professionals including doctors, lawyers and politicians, as well as from high profile Irish personalities. It was not uncommon to see a poem by the Irish children's writer, Patricia Lynch, or a short story by the suffragist and writer, Rosamond Jacob, in the pages of *The Irish Housewife*.[4]

The impressive list of authors who contributed to the magazine is all the more remarkable since they did not receive any payment for their work. In fact, due to a clever arrangement, the production of the magazine did not cost the IHA anything. An advertising agency printed the magazine and in return they received all of the proceeds from the advertising revenue. However, no advertisements were included unless the IHA approved. The inside cover of most issues endorsed any company who advertised in their pages stating that, 'we believe their trading standards to be high, and we ask our readers to support them'. This was a powerful endorsement which companies strived to retain. Each issue originally sold for one shilling and six pence and the IHA kept all of the proceeds from sales.[5] The magazine was therefore a vital source of income and, as Tweedy notes, it functioned to 'distribute information about the Association and recruit members'.[6]

A brief analysis of the content of the magazine points to a radical and engaging publication. Perhaps even more importantly, the magazine offers us an insight into feminist movements from the 1940s to the 1960s in Ireland. This is a time period often neglected by feminist historians. These decades are often incorrectly seen as void of feminist activity in Ireland; after women had secured the vote and before the women's liberation movement was established. The contents of *The Irish Housewife* is therefore an important archive of feminist thought during this time period and a source which has yet to be fully utilised by researchers.[7] This is perhaps best reflected in the first issue of the magazine which contains the final article written by the feminist and nationalist campaigner, Hanna Sheehy Skeffington. By the time the article was published Sheehy Skeffington had died. *The Irish Housewife* thus contributes to the body of writings by this leading feminist activist. The content of the article, 'Random reflections on Housewives; their ways and works', provides us with an insight into feminist concerns of the day. In it Sheehy Skeffington questions:

> what of the large mass of indifferent women who even now fail to realize that Politics control our lives, who shrug and say with coy femininity, 'I don't take any part in Politics, I leave all that to men.' The example of the Housewives has shown that women too must organize, must educate themselves in citizenship, must become vocal, if need be clamorous.[8]

In response to Sheehy Skeffington, the foreword to the same issue describes why women felt the need to establish the Irish Housewives Association. Susan Manning, the first Chair of the IHA, provides an evocative insight into the plight of the Irish housewife in 1940s Ireland.[9] Describing how in search of food:

> ... she travels on crowded buses and waits in queues. Her basket on her arm and a bag in the other hand, she trudges wearily from shop to shop. Too often she finds the prices beyond her means, and has to watch for black marketers, or most 'favoured customers' being supplied from beneath the counter. When on her list is cooked meat, she finds the flies

have arrived first; cooked food is seldom covered. She is served, more often than not, by assistants whose overalls are far from clean and their manners brusque through overtiredness. On her way home she passes through streets littered with orange peel after recurring orange epidemics. She finds the dust bin still unemptied at her door, the rubbish floating around. The baker has called and left a loaf which, quite apart from its natural off-whiteness, needs sending out to the cleaner.[10]

The Irish Housewife did not simply concentrate on the plight of the housewife. The magazine also examined issues pertinent to groups of less fortunate women. In 1948 Katherine Watson undertook visits to female prisoners in Dublin's Mountjoy Jail. Her article, 'Prisons and Women', highlights problems with the legal system in Ireland. She records how:

> in this country 74 per cent of women prisoners are repeatedly committed to short sentences for drunkenness, soliciting, larceny, etc. Such treatment of habitual drunkards is obviously futile as well as expensive; their problem is usually one for the doctor or social worker.[11]

Watson concludes with significant observations that:

> if a prisoner leaves jail feeling deterred and reformed as our penal system has decided that she will, what do we do next? We refuse to give her employment or a passport to leave the country; she is not eligible for unemployment assistance nor, being able-bodied, to enter a County Home. If she wishes to live she is forced to return to her former occupations of stealing, begging or soliciting, and soon she finds that she is one of the recidivists of Mountjoy Jail.[12]

Highlighting the broad and unique range of topics covered in *The Irish Housewife*, on the same page as this hard-hitting article a small table is printed comparing prices for rashers, sausages, tomatoes, eggs and prunes.

The Irish Housewife showcases the vast range of topics with which the IHA were concerned. A reoccurring theme in the magazine was the lack of an adequate system of legal adoption in Ireland. 'Nobody's Child' discusses how the unsuitable system in Ireland in 1950 meant that nothing prevents:

> a child who has been 'adopted' and has grown up happily in his adopted home from being suddenly snatched away from it and placed in an entirely unsuitable environment. Few people are willing to risk the cruel shock this entails for the adopted child and the blow to their own affections.[13]

Republican historian Dorothy Macardle advocated the introduction of legal adoption in Ireland. Her article, 'Chosen Child', was printed in *The Irish Housewife*, asserting that:

> everywhere experts on child welfare have concluded that institutional life is deleterious to children, retarding them in their powers of expression, emotional response, self-confidence and capacity for adaptation to normal social life. Adoption into suitable homes is recognised as much the happiest solution of the friendless child.[14]

The Irish Housewife provides another aspect of interest to the researcher of feminist history. The magazine regularly paid homage to past contributions of women. These articles include vital information on Irish women's accomplishments or simply add interesting facts to our knowledge base. In a tribute to the trade union activist, Louie Bennett, her partner Helen Chenevix describes a ceremony she attended at which a memorial seat was unveiled in St Stephen's Green, Dublin in 1959 by the then female Lord Mayor.[15] The seat, which still takes pride of place in the public park, is inscribed:

> In memory of Louie Bennett, 1870–1956, builder of the Irish Women Workers' Union, Worker for Social Justice, World Peace and the Unity of Ireland. Her sympathy and Love of Humanity knew no Boundaries.

When the painter and stained glass artist Evie Hone died, Stella Frost wrote a detailed account of her life and work. Hone was a highly respected artist of her day. At the height of her success, she was commissioned by the Irish Government to design stained glass windows for the Irish Pavilion at New York World's Fair in 1939. Her windows are now in place at the most prestigious sites including Government Buildings in Dublin and Eton College, Windsor. Frost's article includes an important list of places in Ireland where Hone's stained glass windows can be seen. She concludes that:

> we are too close to Evie Hone's life, and too much shaken by her death, to be able to appreciate herself and her work in their true and lasting colours. We stand like the little figures in a crowd in one of her windows, hushed by a miracle that we barely understand. For her life, and the work she has left to the world and to us, are as near a miracle as we are likely to meet.[16]

The twentieth volume of *The Irish Housewife* appeared in 1966 and in it the IHA celebrated the 'Golden Jubilee' of the 1916 Easter Rising. The cover of the magazine was specially designed by Michael Troughton-Smith. The cover boasts a black and white image of the GPO on O'Connell Street taken in 1966 and a comparison picture taken on Easter Week 1916, after the rebellion had devastated the area. The two photographs are flanked by the colours of the republic; green, white and orange. In the foreword, then Chair of the IHA, Maude Rooney announces:

> We salute the women who took part in this struggle, either actively or by inspiring others. We fear, however, that the women of to-day are so inclined to take independence for granted, that they have become apathetic in their outlook, even to the extent of failing to exercise the franchise properly. We wonder why intelligent women of Ireland are so reluctant to go forward into public life, or to support those few women who do so ... Have the women of 1916 pointed the way all in vain?[17]

The first article in the volume is simply entitled, 'Women of 1916'. The article by Lucy Kingston pays homage to the women who played a role in the Easter Rising, noting that it was not simply men who rebelled but also:

> several outstanding and courageous women, whom it is fitting that we should remember, now fifty years later, when there has been time for many changes in the point of view regarding those exciting days.[18]

She recalls the work of Countess Markievicz, Eva Gore-Booth, Maud Gonne, Grace Plunkett, Helena Molony and Hanna Sheehy Skeffington. Before concluding:

> Ah, but how are the women treated now in the Republic? What has gone wrong in the vision of this generation? Who is to blame? If we had such dedicated fire-brands in our midst to-day – devoted to the *women's* cause, not only the nation's – we might have a better position than the cold reality of the present, where the Republic – whatever its virtues and achievements – is definitely, confessedly and regrettably 'a man's country!'[19]

Articles focusing on serious political issues were often printed alongside recipes for hearty and cheap fare or designs for knitting patterns. Hilda Tweedy regularly contributed to the magazine. Her articles provided consumer information on matters such as Hire Purchase or announced news of IHA campaigns. However, articles were not always of such a serious nature. In one of Tweedy's less formal pieces she describes, with a wry sense of humour, purchasing a new cooker. She announces to readers:

> I could not wait to order my new cooker! The day after the explosion I dashed into town determined to realize my dreams – The explosion? Oh yes, the old one ended with a bang one Sunday evening while the soup was simmering for supper.[20]

Other humorous articles were written by the columnist, Myles na Gopaleen. Brian O'Nolan wrote novels under the pseudonym Flann O'Brien and a satirical column in the *Irish Times* under the name, Myles na gCopaleen. He often reprinted articles from his column, 'Cruiskeen Lawn', for *The Irish Housewife*. In an article written especially for the magazine entitled 'Pots and Pains', na Gopaleen concludes that:

> married life and cookery are almost undistinguishable. If the heart be the seat of love, the stomach next door is its spare room. A husband may patiently endure tantrums, temper, a dirty and damp bed. But cold, wretchedly cooked food? The fat will be in the fire then, and no cookery transaction will be in question![21]

Testimony to the high regard in which *The Irish Housewife* was held, articles by notable Irish personalities often appeared in their pages. In 1950 Anne Yeats, a successful painter and daughter of W.B and George Yeats, published an article to encourage children's creativity. In her piece 'Can Your Child Draw?' she warned, 'don't be too cautious! Beware of all that restricts a child's boldness of hand and of imagination. More is at stake than his future as an artist'.[22] In 1952 the celebrated Irish author and editor, Seán O'Faoláin, contributed an extract from his forthcoming travel book, *An Autumn in Italy*, before it was published by Collins.[23] In 1958 the novelist Kate O'Brien wrote a personal account for the magazine about her birth place, Limerick. O'Brien wrote the article shortly after publication of her novel, *As Music and Splendour*. In the article she describes how:

> when we are young I think that no matter how true our affection for the place of our birth, a strong desire in most of us, many of us, is to travel away from it. Especially if it be a small, or smallish place.[24]

The Irish Housewife was a remarkable publication. Copies of the magazine sold well in shops. Members of the IHA leased stalls at the Spring Show and the Horse Show at the RDS where they successfully sold many copies. However, the advertising market began to slow down in the 1960s and by 1966 it was no longer viable for the advertising agency to print the magazine. After twenty years *The Irish Housewife* ceased publication in 1967. The editorial board did not disband. Tweedy continued to seek alternative methods for the IHA to spread word of their campaigns and to provide vital consumer information. She contacted mainstream women's magazines requesting a page to be given over for IHA news. She suggested a joint endeavour with other women's organisations to produce a communal newsletter or magazine. All of these efforts were to no avail.

In 1972 the IHA established a new editorial board under the chair of Nora Browne. Shortly afterwards a new magazine, *Housewives Voice*, was launched. The magazine was published three times a year and distributed free to members and to the public at recruiting drives. *Housewives Voice* was exchanged with magazines from women's organisations in EEC countries, providing an international exchange of ideas. It ceased publication in 1980. *The Irish Housewife* and *Housewives' Voice* now provide a valuable and engaging archive of Irish feminist thought. A complete collection of these magazines was deposited in the National Archives of Ireland by Hilda Tweedy in 2005, providing a wonderful source which will hopefully be utilised for future research.

This article is dedicated to my favourite 'Irish Housewife', my mother, Marie Tiernan.

NOTES

1   As cited in Fearghal McGarry, *The Rising, Ireland: Easter 1916* (Oxford, Oxford University Press, 2011), p. 30.

2   Hilda Tweedy, *A Link in the Chain: the Story of the Irish Housewives Association 1942–1992* (Dublin, Attic Press, 1992), p. 89.

3   During the final three years of publication, Tweedy is listed as chair or vice chair on the editorial board.

4   Rosamond Jacob, *The Irish Housewife*, 1948, p. 59. Patricia Lynch, *The Irish Housewife*, 1948, p. 27.

5   The price of the magazine was increased in 1960 to two shillings.

6   Tweedy, *A Link in the Chain*, p. 89.

7   The complete run of *The Irish Housewife* and the IHA's subsequent publication, *Housewives Voice*, are held in the Hilda Tweedy collection at the National Archives of Ireland.

8   Hanna Sheehy Skeffington, 'Random reflections on Housewives; their ways and works', *The Irish Housewife*, 1946, p. 22.

9   Susan Manning was sister to union activist, Louie Bennett.

10   Susan Manning, 'Foreword', *The Irish Housewife*, 1946, p. 7.

11   Katherine Watson, 'Prisons and Women', *The Irish Housewife*, 1948, p. 66.

12   *Ibid*, p. 67.

13   A Social Worker, 'Nobody's Child', *The Irish Housewife*, 1950, p. 58.

14   Dorothy Macardle, 'Chosen Child', *The Irish Housewife*, 1950, p. 34.

15   Helen Chenevix, 'In Memory of Louie Bennett', *The Irish Housewife*, 1959, p. 34. The unveiling ceremony was performed by Dublin Lord Mayor, Mrs. Catherine Byrne.

16   Stella Frost, 'Evie Hone', *The Irish Housewife*, 1956, pp 50–7. A complete list of Evie Hone's stained glass windows is printed in D.P. Curran, *Studies*, Summer, 1956.

17   Maude Rooney, 'Foreword', *The Irish Housewife*, 1966, p. 9.

18   Lucy Kingston, 'Women of 1916', *The Irish Housewife*, 1966, p. 15.

19   *Ibid*, p. 18.

20   Hilda Tweedy, 'My New Cooker', *The Irish Housewife*, 1965, p. 75.

21 Myles na Gopaleen, 'Pots and Pains', *The Irish Housewife*, 1963–4, pp 69–70. The title may well have been a comical interpretation of a 1950 article in *The Irish Housewife* entitled 'Pots and Pans'. The article written by P.A. MacMahon focused on cooking utensils suitable for use with electric cookers.

22 Anne Yeats, 'Can Your Child Draw?' *The Irish Housewife*, 1950, p. 68. The article was illustrated by Gillian O'Donovan, aged 6.

23 Seán O'Faoláin, 'An Autumn in Italy', *The Irish Housewife*, 1952, pp 53–5.

24 Kate O'Brien, 'Limerick', *The Irish Housewife*, 1958, p. 56.

Advertisement from *The Irish Housewife*

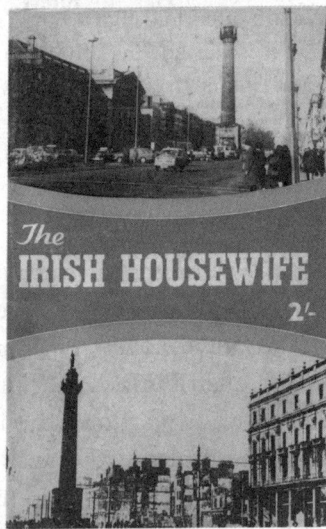

Covers of *The Irish Housewife*, 1950s and 1960s

Putting the Capital H in Housewife:
The Role of the Irish Housewives Association in the Politicisation of Women

Aisling Farrell

We are often told that women's place is the home. We agree that it is her special sphere. But war and social injustice are both enemies of the home. Women and children are their victims as well as men. It is in order to defend the home and the family that women must now take a larger part in public life and politics

– Louie Bennett, 1939.[1]

In early 1941, a group of young married women started a petition seeking the amelioration of the conditions of the poor and unemployed, with particular reference to control over the distribution and pricing of food. Against the background of wartime scarcity and soaring prices, these women sought to supplement the relief work of charitable bodies through the implementation of strategies aimed at provoking government action. Embodying detailed proposals for increasing domestic production and ensuring equitable distribution at fair prices, their petition was to be a direct stimulus for the introduction of government rationing. The interest generated by the 'Housewives Petition' led to the formation of a new organisation for women in the form of the Irish Housewives Association (IHA), whose aim it was:

> to unite women of the house so that they might realise and gain recognition for their right to play an active role in all spheres of planning for the community.[2]

Envisioning their power as a voting bloc, they endeavoured to band housewives into a strong and united force, which would voice the women's point of view and protest against the injustices affecting the home and family. Over a period of decades, the IHA was to bring consumer and women's issues to the centre of Irish political discourse. Firm in their belief that women – in their roles as housewives and mothers – were both directly affected by, and could therefore make a significant contribution to, the economic and political administration of the country, members of the Association therefore organised, demonstrated, lobbied and ran for political office during the middle decades of the twentieth century. In an era of economic convulsions, their activism on issues ranging from profiteering to public policy prompted government officials to assert a greater degree of control over the pricing and distribution of food and other essential commodities.

Much of this work, however, has regularly been discounted as apolitical since many of the issues which moved them to action – rising prices, food shortages, inadequate healthcare facilities and poor housing conditions – have frequently been regarded as 'private sphere' concerns, removed from the centres of power. Even when these women did engage in inarguably political activities such as voting, lobbying, organising demonstrations and deputations, and even planning election campaigns, their sex and status as 'non productive' members of society too often rendered them invisible to the political establishment, thereby enabling their experiences to be interpreted as falling outside the realm of formal political activity.[3] This was a state of affairs which the movement's co-founder, Hilda Tweedy, was keen to rectify when she noted in her pivotal account of the IHA that:

> One of the objects of writing the story of the Irish Housewives Association is to make people aware of the link with the feminist movement of the past. So many people believe that the women's movement was born on some mystical date in the 1970s, like Aphrodite rising from the waves. It has been a long continuous battle in which many women have struggled to gain equality, each generation adding something to the past.[4]

The collection of papers amassed in the Hilda Tweedy archive sheds light on a remarkably broad spectrum of issues in twentieth-century Irish history, and offers important insights into the origins and development of the later women's movement. The purpose of this article is to highlight certain aspects of the IHA's contribution to that process, and to challenge the notion that Irish women, during the decades prior to the 1970s, were capable only of spontaneous protest, but not of any sophisticated or sustained political action.

While it might reasonably be argued that the IHA was, in its early days at least, primarily a home-centred organisation, which defined women's concerns in wider society 'as those which extended their domestic nurturing concerns',[5] even in its early stages the group had always displayed signs of tentative feminist leanings which were to become much more pronounced with the passage of time. This evolution in its political orientation was effectively brought about as a consequence of an understanding that pleas to the government and letters to the press would not always be sufficient to allow them to realise their aims. As its co-founder, Hilda Tweedy, was later to concede, 'we needed committed women in political life, women in the places where the decisions were being made'.[6] It was for this reason that the IHA had decided to endorse the candidature of Hanna Sheehy Skeffington as an Independent candidate for the Dáil in 1943. While supportive of the new group, Hanna had dubious feelings about its title. Writing in the first edition of the association's annual publication, *The Irish Housewife*, in 1946, she expanded on her distaste for 'clumsy man-made words (that) remind us of how little free we really are', pointing out that irony in the fact that the term housewife was still described in legal documents as being:

> 'of no occupation', just as an unmarried woman has to be called a spinster even if she's an architect or Chief Executive and never saw a spinning wheel unless in a museum.[7]

Despite these reservations, however, Hanna was quick to applaud the achievements of 'that band of energetic and determined women' in ending the black market and obtaining price controls. Recognising the Association's potential as a vehicle for bringing women into closer contact with the economic and political spheres, she urged the group to further organisation and education in citizenship, asking:

> What of that large mass of politically indifferent women who even now fail to realise that Politics controls our lives, who shrug and say with coy femininity, 'I don't take any part in Politics, I leave all that to the men.' The example of the Housewives has shown that women *too* must organize, must become vocal, if need be clamorous.[8]

The IHA's feminist credentials were further strengthened in 1947 when it merged with the remnants of the former suffrage movement, the Irish Women Citizens Association (IWCA). An important consequence of this was the formation of the International Sub-Committee of the IHA which was dedicated to carrying on the work of the IWCA through its affiliation to the International Alliance of Women (IAW).[9] Tweedy maintained that the affiliation to the International Alliance of Women 'opened new doors for us and strengthened our feminist convictions'.[10]

In 1949, the IHA was represented for the first time at the IAW Congress held in Amsterdam by Andrée Sheehy Skeffington, Beryl Carr Lett, Ruth Deale and Hilda Tweedy. This was the first time any of the women had been outside of Ireland since 1939 and they were all horrified by the devastation they witnessed in Holland where the process of post-war reconstruction was still underway. They were taken to see the various social services set up to deal with the side effects of the war, and delegates returned from the congress greatly cheered to find that women in other countries were facing the same problems, 'only the emphasis differed', depending on the conditions of women in each country.[11] With 'a renewed enthusiasm', the IHA therefore set about establishing networks to liaise with the commissions of the IAW and to monitor laws and conditions affecting women in Ireland.

Their first step in this regard was to press for equal pay. Representations were made to the government and trade unions, but the only support they received came from the Women's National Council of Action (WNCA), and the Irish Women Workers' Union (IWWU), both of which were chaired by Louie Bennett. Tweedy recounts that they were particularly disappointed by the attitude of the trade unions: 'They just did not want to hear about equal pay'. However, they would soon discover that many of the women themselves had reservations about this issue, as many saw it as a threat to their husbands' livelihoods. She noted that it was the same with other reforms that the IHA sought to initiate: 'women were nervous about innovations; we had to gain their support first'.[12]

To this end, the IHA can be seen to have been actively engaged in continuous efforts to try to shake the political apathy and ignorance of many Irish women, and to demonstrate the impact that politics had on their everyday lives. In her forward to Hilda Tweedy's history of the IHA, Margaret Mac Curtain pointed out that:

> Conscious of the dual role of women in the mid-century they presented to the public the solid frontage of the Irish housewife; strategically they instructed their members on how to negotiate the complex maze of the Irish party machine.[13]

Perhaps nowhere were these efforts more evident than in the Association's journal, *The Irish Housewife*, which circulated between 1946 and 1987. What is particularly striking about this publication is the manner in which articles dealing with such mundane and everyday topics as nutrition and dietetics, rational house design, price and quality control of foodstuffs, were sandwiched in between editorials which often questioned the very economic and political structure of Irish society, and the role of women therein. These writings endeavoured to press upon housewives the fact that the homes in which they worked were intrinsically linked to the fields, shops and offices where their husbands and sons laboured, as well as to the national economy. As Rosaleen Mills noted in the 1951 edition of *The Irish Housewife*:

> To many women in Ireland 'politics' still suggests platitudinous speeches – or worse still, insulting and libellous speeches – and they need to have it brought home to them that 'politics' means the price of food and clothes, the efficiency of schools and hospitals, working conditions for men and women, and in fact, every aspect of our everyday life.[14]

In an article which attempted to assess the significance of the franchise in granting women further access to the power structures of the state, Mills emphasised the need for more women to become active in redressing the gross imbalance of the sexes on both local and national policy-making bodies, pointing out that:

> We can only have a fair proportion of women in public life when voters, especially women voters, urge upon their local committees and party headquarters the desirability of picking suitable women candidates and giving them [their] full support.[15]

The Association's opinions in this regard were not necessarily motivated by a desire to see wives and mothers relieved of their duties in the home, rather they were the assertions of women who found that economic circumstances made it impossible for them to fulfil their responsibilities to the home without taking up the struggle for better conditions through collective action in the public sphere.[16] In this regard, the IHA's activities can be seen to have been very closely allied to those of working-class housewives in America who had mobilised in response to the crisis conditions created by the Great Depression of the 1930s. Understanding their power as a voting bloc, these women had staged food boycotts and anti-eviction protests, created large scale barter networks and lobbied the government for regulation of food prices, housing and utility costs. Many participants also ran for electoral office in numerous localities across the country. In a speech which mirrors the sentiments of Louie Bennett (quoted at the outset of this article), a member of the Farmer-Labor Women's Federation in the United States outlined the motivation behind her movement's activities:

> Women's place may be the home, but the home is no longer the isolated unit it once was. To serve her home best, the woman of today must understand the political and economic foundation upon which that home rests – and then do something about it.[17]

It was as a direct consequence of the desire 'to do something about it' that several members of the IHA

Central Committee decided to mimic the behaviour of their American counterparts by standing in local and national elections. During her period of office as chairwoman Jean Coote stood for election as an Independent to Dublin Corporation in 1950, and the IHA actively campaigned for her, canvassing in her constituency. Though narrowly defeated, she had gained widespread support in many areas and it was felt that if she had had the opportunity to stand again at the next election, she would have had a much greater chance of success. Unfortunately, she passed away in 1953, and the IHA was bereft of a 'most enthusiastic chairwoman who had done so much to train members in procedure and public speaking'. Nevertheless, the campaign had proved a great learning experience for the IHA, and showed what could be achieved with little money but great enthusiasm. Thereafter, the Association began to build up the nucleus of an election fund which it later utilised in order to nominate three of its more experienced members as candidates in the 1957 general election. Throwing the full weight of its support behind the nominees, members of the Association canvassed, handed out leaflets, and even hired a lorry which they then drove through the streets of Dublin addressing crowds through the use of a megaphone. Although none of the candidates were successful, Tweedy felt that the experiment had at least been useful as a means of building up 'a new sense of solidarity amongst members', as well as directing the public's attention to 'the gross imbalance of the sexes in government'. The Association would finally manage to achieve a measure of electoral success in 1966 when it succeeded in having its joint secretary, Carmel Gleeson, elected as a representative of Dublin County Council.[18]

While the IHA itself may have been in no doubt about the need for a greater degree of female participation in public life, much of the Association's press coverage during this period is reflective of the ambivalence with which many sections of the community greeted the idea of politically organised housewives. Both local and national publications took the movement seriously, publishing their letters and details of their deputations and demonstrations. Some of these elements, however, were deeply suspicious about the intentions of this group of housewife activists, and openly questioned the motivation behind some of their activities, often causing considerable turmoil within the organisation. Accusations of communist leanings, for instance, were used on more than one occasion against the IHA by those who did not agree with certain aspects of their work. In 1950, the Association was included among a list of 'communist-dominant' organisations published in *Cavalcade*,[19] while in 1952, an article entitled 'Dangerous Trends in Ireland', published in the *Roscommon Herald*, suggested that the IHA had been involved in rioting in O'Connell Street, and 'had always been used as a medium of expression by Marxists, Communists' and others of a similar outlook.[20] Legal action was taken in both instances, with retractions subsequently being published in the respective newspapers, although in the case of the *Roscommon Herald* this was only achieved after a writ for libel has been issued. Tweedy has noted that these continuous erroneous allegations of communism were:

> extremely upsetting and disruptive for our members, especially in the climate of the time. Not only did it frighten many of our members, but also their husbands who feared that their livelihoods might be affected.[21]

On a number of other occasions, the IHA had also been subjected to quite severe criticism from a watchdog group of social Catholics, operating under the title of 'Vigilans' in *Christus Rex*, a newly-founded journal of sociology, which questioned the representative character of the association, commenting sourly in 1948 that:

> Sometimes I think it would be a good idea if every association had somehow to justify its title before the public, say, by giving membership figures when making public utterances and claims ... Take for instance a body like the Irish Housewives Association and the Irish Women's Progressive League and the (just departed) Irish Women Citizens Association, whose joint secretaries write so many letters to the paper. Do they really represent the women and housewives of Ireland?[22]

The IHA was, by its own admission, a small, primarily Dublin-based, largely Protestant, and essentially middle-class organisation. However, Vigilans' criticisms of the Association were not simply limited to the size and composition of its membership. Castigating the IHA for its recommendations on how to carry on without commercial bakeries during a strike, one member of the Catholic hierarchy stated that they were overlooking the obvious: 'namely, that housewives should bake their own bread. The answer to unsatisfactory capitalist bakeries is not communal bakeries but every home its own bakery'.[23] In what, on the surface, appeared as an attack on the IHA's perceived ideological orientation, in 1949 Vigilans again criticised the IHA for:

> putting over a little propaganda recently in favour of school meals in all the Dublin schools. The occasion, this time, is the report of the National Nutrition Survey ... the form it takes, the usual one of a letter to the press from the joint Honorary Secretaries.[24]

At first glance, the above criticisms can be seen be seen to have been somewhat contradictory, as by the 1950s Catholic social teaching was gradually coming to favour the concept of universal allowances. *Christus Rex* itself published at least one article during this period which warmly supported school meals, infant nurseries for working mothers, and universal health care, while a handbook of Catholic social thought published in 1949 had also been moved to concede that 'the feeding of children in the home is becoming a necessity'.[25] However, as Caitríona Clear has pointed out, when attempting to make sense of the nature and origin of the above attacks it is important to understand that such accusations were, generally speaking, very highly qualified, and it was not so much the overwhelmingly Protestant membership of the organisation that was objected to – nor was it simply its proclivity for advocating communal solutions to domestic orientated problems – rather, what frequently underlay the tone of these objections was the growing tension that these housewife activists were somehow politicising the traditional roles of wives and mothers. The extent of the IHA's activities on the public stage did not rest easily with public perceptions of the role of married women as working away quietly behind the curtain of domesticity, and, as Clear has noted, it was only 'precisely because they were so visible' that concerted efforts were made to see them silenced.[26]

To this end, one of the most important legacies of the IHA's activism was its impact on the political consciousness of the women who took part in the movement. Through participating in public discussions, investigations and deputations, members learned how to speak and write effectively, how to lobby the nation's leaders and to challenge those in positions of power. By organising as consumers, they not only demonstrated a keen understanding of their place in the local and national economic structure, but also shattered the notion that, because homemakers consumed rather than produced, they would automatically be more passive than their wage-earning husbands. Writing in the 1949 edition of *The Irish Housewife*, Rosaleen Mills aptly summed up the manner in which the IHA, through its activities on the public stage, had managed to bring about a change in society's perception of the ordinary housewife:

> The word housewife has typically conjured up a vision of a female body in an apron, bustling about with a sweeping brush, absorbed by the cooking and the darning, whose interest in outside affairs was languid compared to her desire to be assured that we *had* wiped our feet on the mat, or to be informed who had left the bathroom 'in that condition.' The formation of the Irish Housewives' Association, however, revealed that this picture was not the complete housewife. Since this Association has begun to organise the immense latent force that has hitherto been totally inactive in public affairs, it has become usual to write the word Housewife with a capital H.[27]

By breaking through married women's isolation in the home, and encouraging them (as the IHA did) to learn about and become active in changing the world around them, the housewives' movement provided women with a degree of liberation and empowerment, offering them a sense of their own individuality at the same time as it awakened them politically. In this regard, it could be argued that one of the Association's most significant achievements during these years was its success in convincing wives and mothers to present themselves as a legitimate economic and political force, which, like other interest groups such as farmers or trade unionists, could achieve practical gains through a strategy of carefully organised and applied economic pressure. In doing so, whether they intended to or not, they succeeded in politicising the home, the family, and the role of motherhood itself, in important and unprecedented ways.[28]

1   Archive of the Irish Labour History Society, Records of the Irish Women Workers' Union (IWWU), Report of the Executive to the Annual Convention of the IWWU, 3 May 1939.

2   National Archives of Ireland (Hereafter NAI), Hilda Tweedy Papers, 98/17/1/1, Constitution of the Irish Housewives Association, 1946.

3   Linda Connolly, *The Irish Women's Movement: From Revolution to Devolution* (Dublin, Lilliput Press, 2003), pp 72–76.

4   Hilda Tweedy, *A Link in the Chain* (Dublin, Attic Press, 1992), p. 111.

5   Rosemary Cullen Owens, *A Social History of Women in Ireland, 1870–1970* (Dublin, Gill and Macmillan, 2005), p. 295.

6   *Ibid*, p. 46.

7   Hanna Sheehy Skeffington, 'Random Reflection on Housewives – Their Ways and Works', *The Irish Housewife*, Vol. 1, 1946, p. 20.

8   *Ibid.*, p. 22.

9   Charged with safeguarding the individual rights and liberties of all women, the IAW had been instrumental in having the principle of equal rights for men and women included in the 1945 UN Charter. Following on from this victory, in 1947 the Association was granted consultative status as an NGO by the UN Economic and Social Council, thereby endowing its member associations with the responsibility of becoming conduits of reliable information, providing factual data to the UN Secretariat in relation to their experiences in the categories of human welfare and the rights of women in their respective nations. From an Irish point of view, this was a role which was to assume a particular significance during the late 1960s when a directive from the UN Commission on the Status of Women was passed down through the IAW to its constituent societies, encouraging them to examine the status of women in their own countries, and, if necessary, urge their governments to set up a national commission on the subject. See NAI, Hilda Tweedy Papers, 98/17/12/2/1, 'Progress Report', 1949 Congress of the International Alliance of Women, p. 2, and, Tweedy, *A Link in the Chain*, p. 35.

10   Tweedy, *A Link in the Chain*, p. 23.

11   *Ibid.*, p. 27.

12 *Ibid.*, p. 28.

13 *Ibid.*, p. 8.

14 Roseleen Mills, 'The Vote – A Great and Powerful Weapon', *The Irish Housewife*, Vol. 6, 1951, p. 57.

15 *Ibid.*

16 Lucy Kingston, 'Beyond the Home: Some Thoughts on the International Alliance of Women and the Need for Women to Take an Intelligent Interest in World Affairs', *The Irish Housewife*, Vol. 6, 1951, pp 35–36.

17 Annelise Orleck, *Common Sense and a Little Fire: Women and Working Class Politics in the United States, 1900–1965* (North Carolina, The University of North Carolina Press, 1995), p. 218.

18 Tweedy, *A Link in the Chain*, pp 61–62.

19 NAI, Hilda Tweedy Papers, 98/17/1/2/2, Annual Report of the Irish Housewives Association, 1949–50.

20 *Roscommon Herald*, 12 April 1952.

21 Tweedy, *A Link in the Chain*, p. 71.

22 Vigilans, 'As I see it', *Christus Rex*, Vol. 2, 1948, p. 75.

23 *Ibid.*, Vol. 3, 1949, pp 64–65.

24 *Ibid.*, Vol. 4, 1950, pp 74–75.

25 Francis J. Somerville, *Christ is King: A Manual of Catholic Social Doctrine* (Oxford, Catholic Social Guild, 1949), p. 197.

26 Caitriona Clear, *Women of the House: Women's Household Work in Ireland 1922–1961* (Dublin, Irish Academic Press, 2000), p. 39.

27 Rosaleen Mills, 'Housewife', *The Irish Housewife*, Vol. 6, 1949, p. 11.

28 Connolly, *The Irish Women's Movement*, p. 117.

PEACE, GENDER AND HUMAN RIGHTS

Speech given as the Inaugural Hilda and Robert Tweedy Lecture
Trinity College, Dublin
February 2009

Mary Robinson

Thank you Provost, and good morning. It is great to see standing room only in the back of the hall for this lecture and it is a particular pleasure for me to be here. Indeed I have been enjoying this short visit back to Dublin. Yesterday evening a number of us – including some people here today – marked fifty years of women in the Common Room in Trinity, noting that women students were admitted to Trinity in 1904 and then they were allowed to become members of the Common Room in 1958. So there was a gap that we all spoke about last night, and we honoured the four men who were present yesterday evening who actually voted to admit women and they got their moment of thanks from all of us.

Equally being invited to give this inaugural lecture is quite special to me, particularly for the reason that I consider myself a friend of Hilda Tweedy, in particular. I knew her husband Robert slightly because he would come to a number of our meetings, but Hilda is somebody that I am delighted to join, along with all of you, in honouring in this endowed lecture.

I am also delighted to link again with the Centre for Gender and Women's Studies. The centre actually started to work in 1989, but I remember being invited to come for the formal launch as President in 1991. I remember a huge crowd in the atrium and that we were squeezed together. That was a good feeling at the time and a good sense of the future of the centre and I indeed have been following with some pride the way in which the centre has developed.

I am glad to be able to focus on peace, gender and human rights in what I will say in this lecture, because I want to connect my sense of Hilda's contribution to this country with those concepts of peace, gender and human rights and I would like to begin with a quote from Hilda from the 1940s:

> Walk down any street in any town, you will see them, women carrying baskets, bulging string or leather bags, or the latest thing in plastic and zip-fasteners; it doesn't matter which, you will recognise them by their parcels, they are the shopkeepers and the housewives. Whether they housekeep in one room, or own a mansion, their fundamental interests are centred on their homes, and the health and happiness of their families. These women are all feeling the pinch, they are all trying alike to adapt their means to meet the ever increasing cost of living.[1]

That was the way she was capturing the 1940s. There are echoes perhaps of a new reality for many people in the Ireland of today. It was because Hilda was concerned that during the Emergency food was not being distributed equally – there wasn't the fairness she felt was necessary – that she decided she would help organise a petition to the Irish Government. Now in the 1980s, 1990s and in this century it is not so unusual for women to organise a petition to the Government, but at that time in Emergency Ireland – where women were supposed to know their place – it was a major step. It was something that she had the personal moral courage to think of doing and I believe that she was extremely surprised at the response, when some 700, mainly women, signed that petition and she realised that there was an energy there that she could reach out to and capture.

And that was really what gave her the idea, with other women, to form the Irish Housewives Association. There is anecdotal evidence that it was she and Andrée Skeehy Sheffington who choose the name 'Irish Housewives Association' because they felt it represented the place and the space where most women in Ireland dwelled and spent their time. But Andrée's mother-in-law, Hanna Sheehy Skeffington, a noted feminist, is reputed to have said it was a good organisation, but a terrible name! I think that this was captured very well in the foreword to the publication by Hilda Tweedy, *A Link in the Chain: The Story of the Irish Housewives Association 1942–1992* (Attic Press, 1992). In the foreword to that publication Margaret Mac Curtain – the well known historian, known for a long time to a number of us as Sister Ben – points out, and I quote her:

> Over a sustained period of time it has been one of the most influential voices in consumer affairs, monitoring price-controls, lobbying successive governments, and teaching women to play an active role in community affairs as they impinged on economic policy. The Irish Housewives Association while not aligning itself with any particular political party encouraged women to run for office at a period when women's entry into the public sphere had been sharply curtailed.[2]

For Hilda it was a link between the suffrage movement and the contemporary second wave feminist movement. Her contribution and all the energies that she and her contemporaries were bringing together were what I and my contemporaries – a number of whom are here today – were able to follow. I very much felt that we were following in the footsteps of those who had opened up the spaces, who had done so much earlier. In 1948 the Irish Women Citizens' Association, formerly the Irish Women's Suffrage League, was incorporated into the Irish Housewives Association. This made clear the feminist credentials of the IHA and brought it into the International Alliance of Women. Hilda then began to have an international persona, an international career, at this very early stage in the opening up of the women's movement and empowerment here in Ireland. In 1975 she led the Irish delegation to the United Nations meeting in Mexico marking the preparation for International Women's Year. And she was a board member of the International Alliance of Women both in the 1960s and later in the 1970s. She was also a founder member and chairwoman of the Ad Hoc Committee on the Status of Women and then became Chairwoman of the Council for the Status of Women. When the Employment Equality Agency was established in 1977 she was appointed a member by the then Minister of Labour. In other words, in the various ways in which there was new ground being broken, activities, new institutions coming about, Hilda was there; being asked to chair, being asked to be a board member, being asked to be supportive.

Hilda hadn't had an educational link with Trinity as you will see from the very good account of both Hilda and Robert Tweedy in the fine Inaugural Lecture brochure and I compliment the Centre for Gender and Women's Studies on its production. She was educated at Alexandra School – she was a boarder there because her father was a Rector in Alexandria – and then she spent some time in Egypt, married Robert and taught mathematics. But I am very pleased to say in 1990 Dublin University did honour her with an Honorary Degree. It was before my time as

Chancellor but I think it was a recognition of the achievements that she had had throughout her life, as a feminist, as an activist, as an internationalist, but also as a woman who understood that you really make progress in gender equality and women's empowerment if you do it out of the lives of women – the real lives of how women set their own priorities and what they do. For me that was one of the most important contributions that she made. She also helped to write *herstory*, her story, and the Tweedy papers were lodged in the National Archives with records of the Irish Housewives Association from 1941 to 1992 and also records of many of the other organisations that Hilda served on. She understood that the story of the Irish Housewives Association was an important part of Irish history, even if Irish history books weren't really looking in that direction at that time. I think that they now have moved more to understanding the wider social and political history of people and her papers form an honourable component of that story.

When I quoted from Eavan Boland's poetry at my inauguration as President of Ireland, I chose the lines from her poem, 'The Singers', finding a voice, I want women who have been outside history to be written back into history, 'finding a voice where they found a vision'.[3] And Eavan's words summed up at that moment the urgent need I felt to recognise the importance of women in the story of the Irish people and their all too frequent absence from our history. I had a keen sense that poets often find language for what a society is just beginning to understand about itself and at that moment in December 1990 and in the early 1990s things were shifting in Ireland. I think in a way the fact that I was elected President was part of that shift. Eavan Boland's line of poetry using the words 'voice' and 'vision' together suggested the breaking of a long silence and new possibilities for sight and insight. It's crucial to any society that creativity is not held by the few for the few. It grows by being distributed and at that moment in assuming a kind of responsibility to do my best, to do what people asked, to make us proud, as President I had a powerful sense of the long silence of women, breaking and being broken, by poetry, by action, by a commitment to shared purposes. Just as we found language together we found a new understanding of what that language meant and indeed I feel that extraordinarily strongly in the Ireland of now – the issues of participation and language are still there. Our country has changed dramatically. New people have come to our country and become part of our broader sense of identity. The links North and South have been greatly strengthened and we have new voices that must feel free to be heard and new visions to be found.

That brings me to a narrower, more direct focus on the theme of peace, gender and human rights. I think Hilda Tweedy would be pleased with some of the intense focus in recent years in Ireland on addressing the gender based violence which is prevalent in so many parts of the world and which is truly shocking. I have been glad to serve as a mentor if you like, as an encourager, maybe the Irish word *cigire* might be appropriate, of a joint coalition on gender based violence which has been meeting regularly and has an annual meeting that I participate in November each year – we met again last November in the context of a major conference. The joint consortium includes all of the non-governmental organisations that work in developing countries; Trócaire, GOAL, Concern, Oxfam Ireland, Christian Aid, the Irish Red Cross, but it also includes Irish Aid, the Government and the Irish Defence Forces who work in peacekeeping countries and also train peacekeepers. The focus has been very much on tackling gender based violence. And the initiative to establish this joint consortium grew out of a sense of frustration and near despair about the failure to address the level of gender based violence, particularly in Darfur and in the Democratic Republic of Congo. The fact that because there weren't safe spaces, no zero tolerance of gender based violence, women were even more victims of that violence than was in any way to be tolerated and that it was appalling and very frustrating not to be able to tackle it more effectively. Out of those discussions have grown a number of initiatives. First of all, I was encouraged myself to take some of the thinking of this joint consortium and combine with women leaders from different countries, particularly from African countries, and try to be nearer to the women who were suffering this gender based violence at local grassroots level. In September 1997, a group of us went to eastern Chad and we met with women who had fled with their families from Darfur and internally displaced women in Chad and we managed to amplify their voices, to get their voices out, just at the time when European Union countries, including Ireland, were deciding to have a military presence and to help with policing in the camps. As you know that decision was taken and it has been a helpful decision.

I will conclude with this story of another endeavour of women. I think here of women that Hilda Tweedy would have particularly identified with. I think I would like to characterise them as the housewives of Sudan. This was a meeting that took place last month [*January 2009*] in Addis Ababa and again I came with a group of women leaders, who came together and we met with a wonderful organisation called Femmes Africa Solidarité (FAS), headed by a great woman from Senegal called Bineta Diop. Bineta and I have been friends for a number of years and she had asked me to support the second Sudanese Women's Forum on Darfur. When we arrived in Addis we watched as about one hundred women from different parts of Sudan came together in their colourful dress and began to have their preparatory meeting, while we went and had our meeting. The women came from Khartoum, they included women who were quite close to the Sudanese government, but also women who had fled Darfur and were living in Khartoum, the capital, and women even from the south who happened to be living there, so that group had a lot of tension in it. Then we had a group of women from southern Sudan, based in Juba mainly, and they had their own issues. They have had the problems of a long war; they have a tentative peace. They are tentatively part of the government and they have many issues, of poverty, of violence, etc. They had come to focus on the women in Darfur. You had women from the three regions of Darfur; North Darfur, West and South Darfur. One of them, Mona, who was a coordinator of the West Darfur group, spoke at the private meeting of the steering committee on which she sat about her life. She was the first woman in her village to go to university, she still rides a camel locally and she was coordinator of the other women who came from Darfur. She had managed to ensure that one of them was actually a rebel fighter, a woman who was fighting with the rebels who came in as internally displaced from one of the camps. I met that woman and talked to her as well. These women were doing what Hilda Tweedy was talking about in the 1940s, they were determined to change their circumstances. They have come together in a way that the men hadn't been able to and they have formed now a forum with its constitution. They adopted a declaration, they are intending to meet in Darfur hopefully in June and those of us who can have promised to be there with them. We met with the African Union with three of the women from the different regions of Darfur. We just created the space, if you like, for them to meet with the African Union and then they spoke and they made their case. That, I think, is essentially what Hilda Tweedy was about, finding her own voice, learning that when she petitioned the Government, 700 people were also there who felt as she did, that it wasn't fair the way the food was being distributed during the Emergency. She was, I believe, quite right to call it the Irish Housewives Association and to honour that place and space of women of the time. I also think that she would be glad that there is a sense of moving on.

Of course we need to work harder for full gender equality here in Ireland. The Centre for Gender and Women's Studies here, and the other centres in the Universities in Ireland are very very important; the work they do and the research and publications help the next generation. From my point of view what I really like is the linking outwards, the fact that we can also connect and care about those who are terrible victims of violence. Ireland will be participating at an International Women's Symposium in Liberia. Women from Sudan will be coming to tell their story. Ireland will be telling a story that has come out of the gender based violence coalition, that Ireland is developing a plan of action for the Security Council Resolution 1325 which requires that women should be at the peace table, that countries should support this, that every country should have a plan of action. By coincidence Liberia was developing its plan of action, and Ireland and Liberia have taken a unique innovative step of twinning the experiences in both countries. At that conference in November there were women from Liberia and from the other country that we are twinning with, Timor-Leste. When we come to the Symposium in Liberia, this will be an innovative new idea of how women can link. I already know that Finland and Sweden have committed in Liberia to saying they will also start a twinning with other developing countries.

I think that out of the courage and foresight and determination of Hilda Tweedy and her contemporaries there are a lot of issues now where women are trying to be leaders in every sense, coming from the outside to join with the real leaders, who are leading in difficult circumstances to change those circumstances. That is the message that I have always taken from Hilda. She was my friend, but she was also my mentor, and a leader for many of us in the empowerment of women here in Ireland. It is great to see you all here in her honour and in her husband Robert's honour. Thank you very much indeed.

I was remembering that there was one other memory that I did actually intend to end on and I think Hilda would have liked this too. You remember that I ended my inaugural address with Yeats' 'I am of Ireland ... Come dance with me in Ireland'.[4] You know it got me into trouble from time to time! At the end of this serious encounter with the housewives of Sudan, those of us who had come from the outside, which included a few very supportive men, decided on the last evening we would go to this Ethiopian restaurant that somebody had recommended and have a relaxed evening. We heard that the Ambassador of Sudan was having a reception for the Sudanese women and we decided not to feel included – we didn't get any specific invitations, so we let that be for the Sudanese women. So we arrived in the restaurant, a lovely corner was prepared for us for a lovely relaxed evening meal. Lo and behold it was the same restaurant as the ambassador was bringing these hundred Sudanese women! And the ambassador's wife didn't appear too happy that we were there and separate. But then the magic happened. One of our number, who actually leads the women leaders' intercultural forum of my organisation Realizing Rights, was at one stage of her life a professional dancer. So first of all there was formal dancing by very good dancers and musicians in this restaurant which is well known for the quality of it. But then when they retired there was music and some of the Sudanese women got up to dance and immediately Jennifer jumped up and joined them on the floor. Then I realised this was the way that we linked again, so I took the hand of Aisha Ba Diallo, a former Minister of Education of Guinea, and I said 'Aisha, let's dance' and we danced anyway.

NOTES

1   Hilda Tweedy, *The Irish Housewife*, No. 2, 1948.

2   Margaret Mac Curtain, 'Foreword', *A Link in the Chain* (Dublin, Attic Press, 1992).

3   Eavan Boland, 'The Singers', *In a Time of Violence* (Manchester, Carcanet Press, 1994).

4   W.B. Yeats, 'I Am of Ireland', *Words for Music Perhaps* (Dublin, The Cuala Press, 1932).

WHAT CAN THE I.H.A. DO TO HELP YOU?

You have a grievance —

You bring it before the next meeting.

Time is spent in research —

Letters are written to newspapers, government departments etc.

An order is issued —

And life becomes a little easier

IRISH HOUSEWIVES ASSOCIATION
5 Leinster Street, Dublin

I enclose ....Donation/Subscription
to the I.H.A.

Name ....

Address ....

Minimum Annual Subscription 5/-.

Recruitment ad from 1952

STRUGGLING ON ... FEMINISM IS ALIVE AND WELL

Susan McKay

'So many people think that the women's movement was
born on some mystical date in 1970, like Aphrodite rising
from the waves', wrote Hilda Tweedy, explaining why she
was moved to write the story of the Irish Housewives
Association. 'It has', she continued, 'been a long continuous
battle in which many women have struggled to gain
equality, each generation adding something to the
achievements of the past'.

I found it particularly heartening to read this, having
woken up that morning to hear two great Irish feminists,
Nell McCafferty and Margaret Mac Curtain, agree on RTÉ
radio that the second wave of Irish feminism had finished in
the 1980s, unable to survive the bitterness of what Nell once
called 'the war of the womb'. They agreed that maybe some
day feminism might come again, but, for them, it was clear
that Aphrodite had long since sunk back beneath the waves.

Let me make a confession. I am tired of hearing about the
Contraceptive Train. More people will soon be claiming to
have been on that train in 1971 than were in the GPO for the
Easter Rising in 1916. It was a grand and stylish flourish by
great women in a grim time. But it was a magnificent

moment, not the be all and end all. Last year, *The Irish Times* gave it that status, producing a nostalgic supplement on feminism which made the 1970s the glory days and the years since a drab procession.

I came in at what Mac Curtain and McCafferty consider the beginning of the end. I joined the Dublin Rape Crisis Centre as a volunteer in 1979, going on to help set up and then work in the Belfast Rape Crisis Centre in 1982. Everything in my life since then has been informed and coloured by feminism. In the 1990s when, let it be remembered, we finally got divorce, that fine campaigner Cathleen O'Neill commented that 'feminism is alive and well, and fighting for its life'.

It is the normal order of things that the marvellous young will consider themselves more radical, more brave, more effective than the generation of their mothers. Hilda Tweedy acknowledged that the IHA had a problem when it could not attract younger women. The wonderful designer, Joan Bergin, this year won an *Irish Tatler* woman of the year award. In her acceptance speech she urged women to help younger women in every way possible. 'They are nipping at your heels', she said. 'They need our support, and we need them to take over from us'.

Hilda Tweedy was a true radical. She recognised the authority and centrality of women's work within Irish society. She saw the shrewdly-named Irish Housewives Association as a link in a historic chain. She formed alliances with women whose roots were in the suffragette movement, and with those in the new women's liberation movement. She rejected the false division of women into stay at home mothers and workers. She saw the importance of getting onto the international stage, and in using UN instruments to bring about domestic change. She was the first chairperson of the Council for the Status of Women, which went on to become the National Women's Council of Ireland (NWCI).

I have no doubt at all that she would be proud of the Women's Council as it is today, with its paid staff, its almost 200 member organisations, and its extraordinary diversity. We have older women, migrant women, women with disabilities, academic women, trade unionists, artists, business women, women running rape crisis centres and refuges, women in the media; we are supporting a collective of community based women's networks which successfully fought against closure last year. We are campaigning for an end to prostitution, for paid paternity leave, for equal pay. We are struggling with what I call 'retro-sexism', the pervasiveness of pornography, a steep rise in crimes of violence against women. We use the UN and the EU to bring pressure for change in Ireland.

We are working in alliance with women in the North. Our members have elected the first traveller to sit on our board, Tessa Collins, and the first African, Salome Mbugwa, who is our deputy chairperson. We work with brilliant women like Suzy Byrne, aka Maman Poulet, who is revolutionising the lives of women with disabilities through her pioneering use of the new social media. And young women are participating, through the Irish Feminist Network, Cork Feministas and other groupings. One of most exciting and intelligent debates I've ever taken part in was chaired by Mary Robinson in Trinity College soon after I joined the NWCI in 2009. More than 700 students attended, and voted overwhelmingly to defeat a motion proposing that modern Irish women did not need a women's movement.

Feminism is not, however, popular. Nor was it popular in the 1970s. Nor in the 1940s. Poet Adrienne Rich noted in 1981 that feminists faced a serious cultural obstacle, in that each new work was treated as if it emerged from nowhere, with neither historical past nor contextual present. 'So is each contemporary feminist theorist attacked as if her politics were simply an outburst of bitterness or rage', she wrote. General disrespect readily descends into crude abuse. Last year, the owner of one of Ireland's most profitable businesses described feminists who disliked his page 3 pin-up style calendar featuring women from his workforce, as 'ugly women who had no idea how young women empower themselves'.

It has always been a struggle to get women to recognise the need for solidarity with other women, with powerful forces in opposition. Hilda Tweedy recognised this. She wrote about organising the founding meeting of the Irish Housewives Committee in 1942 and wondering if the Irish Women Workers' Union hall would be big enough. 'We need not have worried. Forty turned up and twelve stayed …'. The IHA never had more than 1200 members. Most women, she recognised, 'had neither the time nor the money to attend meetings, and were occupied solely with the mechanics of living'.

It has ever been thus. Poverty dominates the lives of thousands of women in Ireland today, as in the 1940s when the IHA campaigned to protect the poor and the unemployed. The NWCI, in partnership with the Irish Congress of Trade Unions and other NGOs, continues this work. Women still do the lion's share of caring work in Ireland, and the provision of affordable, high quality childcare remains one of Irish feminism's most urgent demands.

It was Sylvia Meehan, veteran of many campaigns for women's equality, who said on International Women's Day 2009 that while feminism has achieved a great deal for women in Ireland, we still do not have political power, and that is what we must get. She is right – there are still more women cleaning Leinster House than serving there as elected representatives, with just 15% of TDs women, some of them women who do not support women's equality.

Violence against women – a critical indicator of women's inequality – is endemic and rising. The women's sector, as it is now known, has suffered disproportionately from funding cuts during the current recession. The funds for our National Women's Strategy, set up in 2007, were ransacked in 2009 to pay for Garda overtime.

Feminists have, nonetheless, got into high places. For the first time in the history of the state we have a female Chief Justice, Attorney General and Director of Public Prosecutions. Susan Denham, Maire Whelan, and Claire Loftus are all women with a record of support for equality. Our former chairperson, Frances Fitzgerald, in her role as Minister for Children, is to introduce legislation giving children rights – and we will support her in what is a truly radical departure for which generations of feminists paved the way.

Minister Fitzgerald, who was involved in setting the agenda for the Second Commission on the Status of Women in 1993, said that many of the items on that agenda still need attention, but her view is that feminism has moved into the mainstream:

> Thousands of women throughout the country now work from a feminist perspective. There is less of the drama of the 1970s and 1980s, but the plodding work is no less essential.

Grainne Healy, who edited Hilda Tweedy's *A Link in the Chain* for Attic Press in 1992, and is also a former chairperson of the NWCI, said that 'going on marches yielded to sitting on committees' in the 1990s, and whereas in the 1970s women staged symbolic invasions of all male domains like the Forty Foot swimming pool, by now women have access to most of the professions, and take their rights to be there for granted. Suzy Byrne said at the launch of the Women's Council's new website in 2009 that new tools like blogging and tweeting can be just as effective as picketing when it comes to campaigning for political change.

Ivana Bacik, a heroine of the fight for women's reproductive rights, is central to the campaign to get more women elected to the Dáil and uses her position as a senator in a highly effective manner. (Ivana seems to have been so important for so long that I asked her once where she was during the 1983 referendum. 'I was in primary school', she replied). Senator Katherine Zappone is a former Women's Council chief executive who is fighting for the rights of gays and lesbians. We have a Minister for Equality who fought in her time for women's social welfare entitlements. Kathleen Lynch told the Women's Council AGM of 2011:

> We really have to start standing up and saying, 'Lads, we're feminists', and the reason you're a feminist is because you believe in equality and it is not something to be ashamed of. There is a great freedom in it.

The election of Michael D Higgins as the 9th President of Ireland is a remarkable triumph for feminism. This is a man who suffered opprobrium and the loss of his Dáil seat because he was on the feminist side in the hard fought referenda of the 1980s. During the presidential campaign we asked all of the candidates if they called themselves feminists:

> Yes, most definitely. Feminism has been a tool for women's empowerment and advancement in many areas, but also for society's progress as a whole.

It was quite wonderful to see at his inauguration, this brave man, flanked by the two women who were presidents before him, Mary McAleese and Mary Robinson, each, in their different ways, formidable feminists.

Hilda Tweedy wrote about the need for feminists to respect one another and work together. I believe that the contemporary women's movement honours her memory in that regard. The 'war of the womb' goes on – 2012 marks the 20th anniversary of the 'X' case, and still no Irish government has had the courage to legislate on the

Supreme Court's ruling. The current government is stalling on implementing the ruling on the A,B,C case in the European Court of Human Rights.

However, we have learned from the bitter battles of the 1980s. We are less confrontational now. I was happy then to chant with my sisters as we stomped down O'Connell Street: 'get your rosaries off our ovaries'. In 2012 I will be happy to sit in the NWCI's handsome new rented offices overlooking that street, discussing with the Irish Family Planning Association how to advance women's right to reproductive health, including the right to choose abortion. After all, 6,000 women a year already do so, although forced to leave this county in secrecy and shame.

Surveys show that a majority of Irish people now quietly support a woman's right to choose abortion in certain circumstances. We accept now, however, that there are decent people who conscientiously oppose it, and that they have a right to hold this view.

Margaret Mac Curtain has wisely said that feminism is more than the women's movement, that it is 'a way of interpreting life [with a] protean quality to its diversities'. Michael D Higgins identifies feminism as a source of the new kind of thinking and imagining that Ireland so badly needs for transformation.

Feminism did not die in the wars of the 1980s, it changed. It changed again in the boom years of the 1990s and it is changing now as this harsh recession hurts women and their aspirations. However, many of the fundamental problems have persisted. Feminism remains crucial to society. Hilda Tweedy emerges from a re-reading of *A Link in the Chain* as a woman whose ideas and practises have considerable contemporary resonance. 'It has been a long hard haul', she wrote in 1992. It still is.

THE

COURT LAUNDRY LTD.

WASHES

*EIDERDOWNS

*PILLOWS

MATS & RUGS

BLANKETS

MOP HEADS

**These can be recovered too*

PHONE —————— 51017

Ad for The Court Laundry, managed by Robert Tweedy

AFTERWORD

Diarmaid Ferriter

I wish people would stop writing cookery and diet books. There are far too many in circulation, most of them spin offs from cheap television shows, haranguing us to be majestic in the kitchen while counting every calorie, or encouraging us to either starve or gorge ourselves into shape. I ignore most of them in favour of a book entitled *Full and Plenty* by Maura Laverty. First published in 1960, it belonged to my wife's grandmother, Hilda Smith, who died in 1995 at the age of 94. The book is full of calories and cream and rich, satisfying dishes, a tribute to a generation of Irish women who believed we should eat a bit of everything natural and wholesome. Obesity was not an issue. These women raised ambitious but sensible children; doers rather than talkers, who embraced change and ambition, but also recognised and admired the strength and resilience of their mothers; their principles and values, and their sheer hard work, including their cooking.

Hilda Smith was a remarkably independent woman who lived on her own for the last twenty years of her life, baking, gardening, going to mass, shopping, spending time with her grandchildren, smiling and rarely complaining. Her motto was simple – everything in moderation. Every time I check something in Laverty's book, I think not only of Hilda Smith, but also of so many Irish women who reach old age, many of them widows, and the fierce independence they demonstrate. They are proud women, many of them stern as well as kind, and rightly bemused, if not disturbed, by the way Ireland has changed. They welcome the fact that women in particular have so much more choice now regarding what to do with their lives. But that does not mean their lives were unfulfilled. Like most of her generation, Hilda Smith was a housewife for forty years. That was her job, and she was brilliant at it. Being a housewife for that long did not mean her life was one of drudgery, no rewards, no independence and a lack of opinions or views.

In the summer of 2005 there was a battle for the title 'Ireland's greatest woman' on Marian Finucane's RTÉ radio show. It threw up characters many were familiar with, but also some who many listeners would not have heard of. One woman who was briefly acknowledged was Hilda Tweedy, a founding member of the Irish Housewives Association (IHA), who died in 2005 at the age of 93.

In 2003, I had the privilege of listening to Tweedy when she presented the archive of the IHA to the National Archives of Ireland. Even towards the end of a long and active life, she was exceptionally mentally agile, and spoke strongly and unscripted. The presentation of the papers to the state archives was an important step in ensuring that the IHA receives adequate recognition from historians and those attempting to write a history of the Irish women's movement. To many, the IHA would not be regarded as an organisation that deserves a place in the feminist hall of fame; after all, the word 'housewife' tends now to be derided, and some contemporary housewives have taken to labelling themselves 'social engineers' or 'domestic managers'.

This is understandable in a politically correct age, but the cleverness of Tweedy and others in politicising the term 'housewife' in the 1940s and 1950s in order to effect real improvement in the lives of Irish women should not be underestimated. The original Housewives Petition, drawn up and sent to the government in May 1941, and which formed the basis of the establishment of the IHA, dealt with themes that have had an enduring relevance for Irish society, such as price control of essential goods, affordable fuel and a demand for school meals and welfare schemes for mothers and children. They were also the first organisation to present housewives as consumers and not just passive breeders and feeders.

As Rosaleen Mills, an IHA activist who worked with Tweedy, wrote in 1949:

> Since this association has begun to organise the immense latent force that has hitherto been totally inactive in public affairs, it has become usual to write the word Housewife with a capital H. To the man in the street she has come to mean the person who constantly chivvies the Powers that Be, from Merrion Street to Moore Street, on the question of the cost of living and the everyday problems of everyday people. To the producer and worker she has come to mean a consumer who wants and appreciates the best, and who is anxious to see the producer and the middleman get a fair deal for fair service.

In 1957, the IHA unsuccessfully contested four constituencies in the general election, a measure of the difficulties in making a breakthrough in national politics. But the association was determined to monitor legislation affecting women and children, and Tweedy was a founding member and Chairwoman of the Ad Hoc

Committee that was responsible for the formation of the Commission on the Status of Women in 1970.

Tweedy and her colleagues thus provided a crucial link between the female activists of the 1940s and the 1950s and the Women's Liberation Movement of subsequent decades, a reminder of the inadequacy of a historical assessment of the women's movement that leaps straight from the suffrage campaign to the condom train.

The IHA were, of course, operating in a hostile climate. The egalitarianism of the rhetoric of the 1916 Proclamation had been jettisoned; as indeed (and this is often forgotten) had Article 3 of the Irish Constitution of 1922 which promised equality to 'every person without distinction of sex'. De Valera omitted this from the 1937 Constitution in favour of Article 41, which refers to a woman's 'life within the home' as the basis for common good. Tweedy and her colleagues sought to make this a political issue, and in doing so, exposed the hypocrisy and class-consciousness of Irish society. They not only encouraged women to take up training for themselves and their daughters in order to take jobs outside of the home, but also demanded an equitable healthcare system, affordable housing, decent conditions in national schools, and highlighted the extent to which people were being ripped off for basic goods and services, long before Eddie Hobbs appeared.

Their campaigns exposed the inadequacy of the political establishment in finding solutions to these basic problems in a society that supposedly cherished the sanctity of the home, of women and of children. In one interview, Tweedy recalled leading a deputation of the IHA to Dublin Corporation asking for school meals, only to be informed that 'we were breaking the sanctity of the home', as corporation officials painted an idyllic and utterly unrealistic picture of the whole family sitting around a table at lunchtime. As Tweedy pointed out, nobody seemed to worry about the sanctity of the home when they sent children who should have been at school out to work, or when well-off parents sent children to boarding school, and 'nobody worried about charladies and others who were going out to do a day's work'.

Tweedy represented an important generation of Irish women whose commitment to their communities stood in stark contrast to the empty rhetoric and blatant class discrimination practised by their male political masters. The archive Hilda Tweedy bestowed to the state should ensure that the efforts of the IHA will not be forgotten, just as Hilda Smith's well-thumbed copy of *Full and Plenty* sitting on our kitchen shelf will ensure her legacy endures.

CAITRÍONA CLEAR lectures in modern Irish and European history at the National University of Ireland, Galway and is one of the pioneering generation of scholars of Irish women's history. Among her publications are *Nuns in Nineteenth Century Ireland* (Gill and Macmillan/Catholic University of America Press, 1987/1988), *Women of the House: Women's Household Work in Ireland, 1922–1961* (Irish University Press, 2000) and *Social Change and Everyday Life in Ireland, 1850–1922* (Manchester University Press, 2007).

MARY CULLEN is one of Ireland's leading historians. She was, in 1967, the first female member of academic staff employed by Maynooth University and played a key role in developing their world-class History Department. In 2011 Maynooth conferred her with an Honorary Doctorate of Literature. Among her publications are *Girls Don't Do Honours: Irish Women in Education in the Nineteenth and Twentieth Centuries* (Arlen House, 1987); *Women, Power and Consciousness in Nineteenth-Century Ireland* (Attic Press, 1995); *1798: 200 Years of Resonance* (Irish Reporter Publications, 1998); *Female Activists: Irish Women and Change 1900–1960* (Woodfield Press, 2001) and *Telling it Our Way: Essays in Gender History* (Arlen House, 2012).

ROSEMARY CULLEN OWENS holds an MA in Modern Irish History from University College, Dublin, and a Higher Diploma in education from Trinity College, Dublin. Her research speciality is the history of Irish women from 1870, allied to the effect of contemporary developments on women, including the labour, nationalist and pacifist movements. Among her publications are: *Smashing Times: A History of the Irish Women's Suffrage Movement 1889–1922* (Dublin, Attic Press, 1984/1995), *Louie Bennett: A Biography* (Cork, Cork University Press, 2001) and *A Social History of Women in Ireland 1870–1970* (Dublin, Gill and Macmillan, 2005).

BRYCE EVANS is Lecturer in Modern History at Liverpool Hope University. A graduate of the University of Warwick and the NUI, his doctoral dissertation focused on the black market in Ireland during the Second World War. His most recent publication was a critical biography of former Taoiseach Seán Lemass, subtitled *Democratic Dictator* (Collins Press, 2011).

AISLING FARRELL is a graduate of St. Patrick's College, Drumcondra (Dublin City University) where she is currently completing a Ph.D. assessing the aims and activities of a variety of women's organisations in Ireland during the period in between enfranchisement and the rise of the modern women's movement. This research has been funded by the Irish Research Council for the Humanities and Social Science's Postgraduate Scholarship Scheme.

DIARMAID FERRITER is Professor of Modern Irish History at UCD. His main research interests are the social, political and cultural history of twentieth century Ireland. Among his books are *Occasions of Sin: Sex and Society in Modern Ireland* (London, Profile Books, 2009), *Judging Dev: A Reassessment of the Life and Legacy of Éamon de Valera* (Dublin, Royal Irish Academy, 2007), *The Transformation of Ireland, 1900–2000* (London, Profile Books, 2004), *Lovers of Liberty? Local Government in Twentieth Century Ireland* (Dublin, National Archives of Ireland, 2001) and, with Colm Tóibín, *The Irish Famine: A Documentary* (London, Profile Books, 2001).

ALAN HAYES is publisher and editor of Arlen House; a member of the Management Team of Dublin UNESCO City of Literature; founder of the Dublin Book Festival and its artistic director, 2008–2010. Among his publications are *The Years Flew By* (Arlen House, 2000); *The Irish Women's History Reader* (Routledge, 2000); *Irish Women's History* (Irish Academic Press, 2004); *Cúirt 21* (Cúirt, 2006); *Pauline Bewick at 75: A Photo Biography* (Arlen House, 2010). He is currently working on *"John Brennan" and Her Sisters*, and a history of Irish feminist publishing.

MARGARET MAC CURTAIN is one of Ireland's most acclaimed historians. Over the past half century she has built an internationally lauded academic career, while also developing many innovative education initiatives at both second and third level, and engaging enthusiastically with the women's movement, in Ireland and internationally. Among her many publications are *Tudor and Stuart Ireland* (Gill and Macmillan, 1971), *Women in Irish Society: The Historical Dimension* (Arlen House, 1978), *Women in Early Modern Ireland* (Edinburgh University Press/Wolfhound, 1991), *The Field Day Anthology of Irish Writing: Volumes 4 and 5: Irish Women's Writing and Traditions* (Cork University Press, 2002) and *Ariadne's Thread: Writing Women into Irish History* (Arlen House, 2008).

SUSAN MCKAY is Chief Executive of the National Women's Council of Ireland and a regular media contributor on politics, the arts and women's issues. Among her publications are *Sophia's Story* (Gill and Macmillan, 1998/2004), *Northern Protestants: An Unsettled People* (Blackstaff Press, 2000/2005), *Without Fear: 25 Years of the Dublin Rape Crisis Centre* (New Island, 2005) and *Bear in Mind These Dead* (Faber, 2008).

MARY ROBINSON is President of the *Mary Robinson Foundation – Climate Justice*. She served as President of Ireland from 1990–1997 and UN High Commissioner for Human Rights from 1997–2002. She is a member of the *Elders* and the *Club of Madrid* and the recipient of numerous honours and awards including the *Presidential Medal of Freedom* from the President of the United States Barack Obama. A former President of the *International Commission of Jurists* and former chair of the *Council of Women World Leaders* she was President and founder of *Realizing Rights: The Ethical Globalization Initiative* from 2002–2010. Mary Robinson serves as Honorary President of *Oxfam International* and Chair of Board of the *Institute of Human Rights and Business* in addition to being a board member of several organisations including the *Mo Ibrahim Foundation* and the *European Climate Foundation*. Mary is the Chancellor of the *University of Dublin* since 1998.

MARY RYAN is Assistant Principal in Castleknock Community College, Dublin. Her work as an EAL (English as an Additional Language) teacher has brought her into the Ireland of multiculturalism and plurilingualism. She chaired the Dublin 15 Schools Cultural Mediation Project and Pathways to Parental Involvement, a training programme for immigrant parents and was a member of the National Advisory Board of the Immigrant Council of Ireland which developed a Toolkit for Migrant Parents. She established Grandparents' Day in School which is now a national project; edited *No Shoes in Summer* (Wolfhound, 1995), Ireland's first third age anthology and coordinated *Golden Reels*, Ireland's first third age film festival.

SONJA TIERNAN is a Teaching Fellow in the Department of Politics, History, Media and Communication at Liverpool Hope University, UK. Her past awards include the National Endowment of the Humanities Fellowship at the Keough-Naughton Institute for Irish Studies, University of Notre Dame (2010–11) and the Government of Ireland Post-Doctoral Research Fellowship (2008–10), which she conducted in the School of Histories and Humanities at Trinity College, Dublin. Her latest book, *Eva Gore-Booth: An Image of Such Politics* will be published by Manchester University Press in 2012. Sonja is Secretary of the Women's History Association of Ireland and curator of the Hilda Tweedy exhibition.

MARYANN VALIULIS is Director of the Centre for Gender and Women's Studies at Trinity College, Dublin. Her research interests include the role of women in society and politics in twentieth century Ireland and continental Europe; women's history and women's studies. Among her publications are *Gender Balance and Gender Bias in Education: International Perspectives* (Routledge, 2010); *Gender and Power in Irish History* (Irish Academic Press, 2008); *Gender and Sexuality in Modern Ireland* (University of Massachusetts Press, 1997); *Women and Irish History* (Wolfhound Press, 1997); *Portrait of a Revolutionary: General Richard Mulcahy and the Founding of the Irish State* (University Press of Kentucky/Irish Academic Press, Dublin, 1992).

Thanks to the Tweedy family for their support of the Hilda Tweedy centenary events and for providing financial support towards the Hilda Tweedy Exhibition and Symposium at Trinity College, Dublin in November 2011. I would like to acknowledge the enthusiasm, energy and hard work of Dr Jean Walker, Hilda's youngest daughter.

Many thanks to Hilda's friends, Dr Margaret Mac Curtain, Mary Ryan, Rosemary Cullen Owens, Dr Mary Cullen, Dr Mary Robinson and Jean Mullen, for their support.

It has been a privilege to work on the Hilda Tweedy Centenary events with Dr Maryann Valiulis, Dr Sonja Tiernan, Catriona Crowe, Ger Garland and Louise McCaul. I'd like to express my appreciation to my colleagues in Dublin UNESCO City of Literature, Dublin Public Libraries, Dublin City Council and Culture Ireland for their support.

Special thanks to Siobháin Brophy, Simon Williams, Belinda Clements, Dr Mary McAuliffe, The Irish Times, Professor Brian Ó Conchubhair and Mairead McLoughlin.

Advertisement from *The Irish Housewife*